A Global Ethic and

A Global Ethic and Global Responsibilities

Two Declarations

Edited by Hans Küng
and Helmut Schmidt

with a preface by
The Right Honourable the Lord Menuhin,
OM, KBE

SCM PRESS LTD

Translated from *Erklärung zum Weltethos.*
Die Deklaration des Parlaments der Weltreligionen,
published 1993 by R. Piper GmBH & Co KG, Munich,
and *Allgemeine Erklärung der Menschenpflichten,*
published 1998 by R. Piper GmBH & Co KG, Munich.

© 1993, 1998 by R. Piper GmBH & Co KG, Munich.

Where there is no already existing English text,
translation © John Bowden 1993, 1998.

0 334 02740 3

First published 1998 by
SCM Press Ltd
9–17 St Albans Place, London N1 0NX

Typeset by Regent Typesetting, London
and printed in Great Britain
by Biddles Ltd, Guildford and King's Lynn

Contents

v

Preface by the Right Honourable the Lord Menuhin, OM, KBE

I have found profound encouragement for human advance in this Declaration of Human Responsibilities. It is in a way the first assertion of human dignity. The claim to human rights is generally made on behalf of those many denied human rights. The responsibilities are exercised by the fewer, often at the expense of human rights. Therefore, a new dignity, inalienable to each individual, group or culture, is recognized: the dignity of the responsible one, the one in charge, the momentarily stronger – the dignity of responsibility.

The responsibility of the responsible, the rights of the dependent; this is the right way. Often we face the wrong way, i.e. the abused rights of the responsible, the lack of rights and the responsibilities of the dependent.

This document, which corrects a flawed form of thinking, should be adopted by all institutions in the free world and taught in every school, and introduced into every society of exclusion. It can serve as a measure for the civilizing process in humanity. It is indeed the first time that we all have a really workable common denominator for all human life under whatever flag, allegiance, or faith it may exist.

Humanity and, in fact, all life on earth is crying for a voice which will carry moral authority. This is an authority without which our laws – and even international laws – can never exercise their mandated functions, for law depends in the final analysis on general consensus.

We need to agree on at least this one self-evident truth, this axiom, that humanity will never progress humanly unless we all recognize that human rights can never exist without human responsibilities. They form one coin. It is the one and only universal currency for true human exchange, it is firm and stable. It will protect us from wars, civil wars – all wars are becoming ever more 'civil' as we acknowledge our inter-dependence – from human exploitation, from misery, economic disaster, and will, in fact, strengthen human rights, not to speak of human trust, human thinking, human happiness.

As we are possessed by the Infinite and the Eternal, as every cell and every atom is for ever propelled and attracted to an ever higher enlightenment, the acknowledgment of obligation in return for the freedom of learning and giving draws us to our innermost religious nature – compatible with religious expression, whether Christian, Jewish, Buddhist, animist, or even pagan, as in Greece.

Man is by definition a religious, a moral animal, even in madness, but redeemable.

Yehudi Menuhin   10 April 1998

The Declarations

A Universal Declaration of Human Responsibilities proposed by the InterAction Council

1 September 1997

Introductory Comment

It is time to talk about human responsibilities

Globalization of the world economy is matched by global problems, and global problems demand global solutions on the basis of ideas, values and norms respected by all cultures and societies. Recognition of the equal and inalienable rights of all the people requires a foundation of freedom, justice and peace – but this also demands that rights and responsibilities be given equal importance to establish an ethical base so that all men and women can live peacefully together and fulfil their potential. A better social order both nationally and internationally cannot be achieved by laws, prescriptions and conventions alone, but needs a global ethic. Human aspirations for progress can only be realized by agreed values and standards applying to all people and institutions at all times.

Next year will be the 50th anniversary of the Universal Declaration of Human Rights adopted by the United Nations. The anniversary would be an opportune time to adopt a Universal Declaration of Human Responsibilities, which would complement the Human Rights Declaration and strengthen it and help lead to a better world.

The following draft of human responsibilities seeks to bring freedom and responsibility into balance and to

The Declaration of the Parliament of the World's Religions

Introduction

The world is in agony. The agony is so pervasive and urgent that we are compelled to name its manifestations so that the depth of this pain may be made clear. Peace eludes us ... the planet is being destroyed ... neighbours live in fear ... women and men are estranged from each other ... children die! *This is abhorrent!*

We condemn the abuses of Earth's ecosystems. We condemn the poverty that stifles life's potential; the hunger that weakens the human body; the economic disparities that threaten so many families with ruin. We condemn the social disarray of the nations; the disregard for justice which pushes citizens to the margin; the anarchy overtaking our communities; and the insane death of children from violence. In particular we condemn aggression and hatred in the name of religion. *But this agony need not be.*

It need not be because the basis for an ethic already exists. This ethic offers the possibility of a better individual and global order, and leads individuals away from despair and societies away from chaos.

We are women and men who have embraced the precepts and practices of the world's religions. We affirm that a common set of core values is found in the teachings of the religions, and that these form the basis of a global ethic. We affirm that this truth is already known, but yet to be lived in heart and action. We affirm that there is an irrevocable, unconditional norm for all areas of life, for families and communities, for races, nations and religions. There already exist ancient guidelines for human behaviour which are found in the teachings of the religions of the world and which are the conditions for a sustainable world order.

We declare: We are interdependent. Each of us depends on the

3

promote a move from the freedom of indifference to the freedom of involvement. If one person or government seeks to maximize freedom but does it at the expense of others, a larger number of people will suffer. If human beings maximize their freedom by plundering the natural resources of the earth, then future generations will suffer.

The initiative to draft a Universal Declaration of Human Responsibilities is not only a way of balancing freedom with responsibility, but also a means of reconciling ideologies, beliefs and political views that were deemed antagonistic in the past. The proposed declaration points out that the exclusive insistence on rights can lead to endless dispute and conflict, that religious groups in pressing for their own freedom have a duty to respect the freedom of others. The basic premise should be to aim at the greatest amount of freedom possible, but also to develop the fullest sense of responsibility that will allow that freedom itself to grow.

The InterAction Council has been working to draft a set of human ethical standards since 1987. But its work builds on the wisdom of religious leaders and sages down the ages who have warned that freedom without acceptance of responsibility can destroy the freedom itself, whereas when rights and responsibilities are balanced, then freedom is enhanced and a better world can be created.

The InterAction Council commends the following draft Declaration for your examination and support.

well-being of the whole, and so we have respect for the community of living beings, for people, animals, and plants, and for the preservation of Earth, the air, water and soil. We take individual responsibility for all we do. All our decisions, actions, and failures to act have consequences.

We must treat others as we wish others to treat us. We make a commitment to respect life and dignity, individuality and diversity, so that every person is treated humanely, without exception. We must have patience and acceptance. We must be able to forgive, learning from the past but never allowing ourselves to be enslaved by memories of hate. Opening our hearts to one another, we must sink our narrow differences for the cause of world community, practising a culture of solidarity and relatedness.

We consider humankind our family. We must strive to be kind and generous. We must not live for ourselves alone, but should also serve others, never forgetting the children, the aged, the poor, the suffering, the disabled, the refugees, and the lonely. No person should ever be considered or treated as a second-class citizen, or be exploited in any way whatsoever. There should be equal partnership between men and women. We must not commit any kind of sexual immorality. We must put behind us all forms of domination or abuse.

We commit ourselves to a culture of non-violence, respect, justice and peace. We shall not oppress, injure, torture, or kill other human beings, forsaking violence as a means of settling differences. We must strive for a just social and economic order, in which everyone has an equal chance to reach full potential as a human being. We must speak and act truthfully and with compassion, dealing fairly with all, and avoiding prejudice and hatred. We must not steal. We must move beyond the dominance of greed for power, prestige, money, and consumption to make a just and peaceful world. Earth cannot be changed for the better unless the consciousness of individuals is changed first. We pledge to increase our awareness by disciplining our minds, by meditation, by prayer, or by positive thinking. Without risk and a readiness to sacrifice there can be no fundamental change in our situation. Therefore we commit ourselves to this global ethic, to understanding one another, and to socially-beneficial, peace-fostering, and nature-friendly ways of life.

We invite all people, whether religious or not, to do the same.

A Universal Declaration of Human Responsibilities
(proposed by the InterAction Council)

Preamble

Whereas recognition of the inherent dignity and of the equal and inalienable rights of all members of the human family is the foundation of freedom, justice and peace in the world and implies obligations or responsibilities,

whereas the exclusive insistence on rights can result in conflict, division, and endless dispute, and the neglect of human responsibilities can lead to lawlessness and chaos,

whereas the rule of law and the promotion of human rights depend on the readiness of men and women to act justly,

whereas global problems demand global solutions which can only be achieved through ideas, values, and norms respected by all cultures and societies,

whereas all people, to the best of their knowledge and ability, have a responsibility to foster a better social order, both at home and globally, a goal which cannot be achieved by laws, prescriptions, and conventions alone,

whereas human aspirations for progress and improvement

6

The Declaration of the Parliament of the World's Religions

The Principles of a Global Ethic

Our world is experiencing a *fundamental crisis:* a crisis in global economy, global ecology, and global politics. The lack of a grand vision, the tangle of unresolved problems, political paralysis, mediocre political leadership with little insight or foresight, and in general too little sense for the commonweal are seen everywhere. Too many old answers to new challenges.

Hundreds of millions of human beings on our planet increasingly suffer from unemployment, poverty, hunger, and the destruction of their families. Hope for a lasting peace among nations slips away from us. There are tensions between the sexes and generations. Children die, kill, and are killed. More and more countries are shaken by corruption in politics and business. It is increasingly difficult to live together peacefully in our cities because of social, racial, and ethnic conflicts, the abuse of drugs, organized crime, and even anarchy. Even neighbours often live in fear of one another. Our planet continues to be ruthlessly plundered. A collapse of the ecosystem threatens us.

Time and again we see leaders and members of *religions* incite aggression, fanaticism, hate, and xenophobia – even inspire and legitimate violent and bloody conflicts. Religion often is misused for purely power-political goals, including war. We are filled with disgust.

We condemn these blights and declare that they need not be. An *ethic* already exists within the religious teachings of the world which can counter the global distress. Of course this ethic provides

7

can only be realized by agreed values and standards applying to all people and institutions at all times,

Now, therefore,

The General Assembly

proclaims this Universal Declaration of Human Responsibilities as a common standard for all peoples and all nations, to the end that every individual and every organ of society, keeping this Declaration constantly in mind, shall contribute to the advancement of communities and to the enlightenment of all their members. We, the peoples of the world, thus renew and reinforce commitments already proclaimed in the Universal Declaration of Human Rights: namely, the full acceptance of the dignity of all people; their inalienable freedom and equality, and their solidarity with one another. Awareness and acceptance of these responsibilities should be taught and promoted throughout the world.

no direct solution for all the immense problems of the world, but it does supply the moral foundation for a better individual and global order: a vision which can lead women and men away from despair, and society away from chaos.

We are persons who have committed ourselves to the precepts and practices of the world's religions. We confirm that there is already a consensus among the religions which can be the basis for a global ethic – a minimal *fundamental consensus* concerning binding *values*, irrevocable *standards*, and fundamental *moral attitudes*.

I. No new global order without a new global ethic

We women and men of various religions and regions of Earth therefore address all people, religious and non-religious. We wish to express the following convictions which we hold in common.

- We *all* have a *responsibility for a better global order*.
- Our involvement for the sake of human rights, freedom, justice, peace, and the preservation of Earth is absolutely necessary.
- Our different religious and cultural traditions must not prevent our common involvement in opposing all forms of inhumanity and working for greater humaneness.
- The principles expressed in this global ethic can be affirmed by all persons with ethical convictions, whether religiously grounded or not.
- As *religious and spiritual* persons we base our lives on an Ultimate Reality, and draw spiritual power and hope therefrom, in trust, in prayer or meditation, in word or silence. We have a special responsibility for the welfare of all humanity and care for the planet Earth. We do not consider ourselves better than other women and men, but we trust that the ancient wisdom of our religions can point the way for the future.

After two world wars and the end of the cold war, the collapse of fascism and nazism, the shaking to the foundations of communism and colonialism, humanity has entered a new phase of its history. Today we possess sufficient economic, cultural, and spiritual resources to introduce a better global order, but old and new *ethnic, national, social, economic, and religious tensions* threaten the peaceful building of a better world. We have experienced greater

9

technological progress than ever before, yet we see that world-wide poverty, hunger, death of children, unemployment, misery, and the destruction of nature have not diminished but rather have increased. Many peoples are threatened with economic ruin, social disarray, political marginalization, ecological catastrophe, and moral collapse.

In such a dramatic global situation humanity needs a *vision of peoples living peacefully together*, of ethnic and ethical groupings and of religions sharing responsibility for the care of Earth. A vision rests on hopes, goals, ideals, standards. But all over the world these have slipped from our hands. Yet we are convinced that, despite their frequent abuses and failures, it is the communities of faith who bear a responsibility to demonstrate that such hopes, ideals, and standards can be guarded, grounded and lived. This is especially true in the modern state. Guarantees of freedom of conscience and religion are necessary, but they do not substitute for binding values, convictions, and norms which are valid for all humans regardless of their social origin, sex, skin colour, language, or religion.

We are convinced of the fundamental unity of the human family on Earth. We recall the 1948 Universal Declaration of Human Rights of the United Nations. What it formally proclaimed on the level of *rights* we wish to confirm and deepen here from the perspective of an *ethic*: the full realization of the intrinsic dignity of the human person, the inalienable freedom and equality in principle of all humans, and the necessary solidarity and interdependence of all humans with each other.

On the basis of personal experiences and the burdensome history of our planet we have learned

- that a better global order cannot be created or enforced by laws, prescriptions, and conventions alone;
- that the realization of peace, justice, and the protection of earth depends on the insight and readiness of men and women to act justly;
- that action in favour of rights and freedoms presumes a consciousness of responsibility and duty, and that therefore both the minds and hearts of women and men must be addressed;
- that rights without morality cannot long endure, and that there will be *no better global order without a global ethic*.

By a *global ethic* we do not mean a global ideology or a *single*

11

Fundamental Principles for Humanity

Article 1

Every person, regardless of gender, ethnic origin, social status, political opinion, language, age, nationality, or religion, has a responsibility to treat **all people in a humane way.**

unified religion beyond all existing religions, and certainly not the domination of one religion over all others. By a global ethic we mean a *fundamental consensus on binding values, irrevocable standards, and personal attitudes.* Without such a fundamental consensus on an ethic, sooner or later every community will be threatened by chaos or dictatorship, and individuals will despair.

II. A fundamental demand: Every human being must be treated humanely

We all are fallible, imperfect men and women with limitations and defects. We know the reality of evil. Precisely because of this, we feel compelled for the sake of global welfare to express what the fundamental elements of a global ethic should be – for individuals as well as for communities and organizations, for states as well as for the religions themselves. We trust that our often millennia-old religious and ethical traditions provide an *ethic* which is convincing and practical for *all women and men of good will*, religious and non-religious.

At the same time we know that our various religious and ethical traditions often offer very different bases of what is helpful and what is unhelpful for men and women, what is right and what is wrong, what is good and what is evil. We do not wish to gloss over or ignore the serious differences among the individual religions. However, they should not hinder us from proclaiming publicly *those things which we already hold in common* and which we jointly affirm, each on the basis of our own religious or ethical grounds.

We know that religions cannot solve the environmental, economic, political, and social problems of Earth. However, they can provide what obviously cannot be attained by economic plans, political programmes or legal regulations alone: *a change in* the inner orientation, the whole mentality, *the 'hearts' of people*, and a conversion from a false path to a new orientation for life. Humankind urgently needs social and ecological reforms, but it needs spiritual renewal just as urgently. As religious or spiritual persons we commit ourselves to this task. The spiritual powers of the religions can offer a fundamental sense of trust, a ground of meaning, ultimate standards, and a spiritual home. Of course religions

Article 2

No person should lend support to any form of inhumane behaviour, but all people have a responsibility to strive for the dignity and self-esteem of all others.

Article 3

No person, no group or organization, no state, no army or police stands above good and evil; all are subject to ethical standards. Everyone has a responsibility to promote good and to avoid evil in all things.

Article 4

All people, endowed with reason and conscience, must accept a responsibility to each and all, to families and communities, to races, nations, and religions in a spirit of solidarity: **What you do not wish to be done to yourself, do not do to others.**

are credible only when they eliminate those conflicts which spring from the religions themselves, dismantling mutual arrogance, mistrust, prejudice, and even hostile images, and thus demonstrate respect for the traditions, holy places, feasts, and rituals of people who believe differently.

Now as before, *women and men are treated inhumanely* all over the world. They are robbed of their opportunities and their freedom; their human rights are trampled underfoot; their dignity is disregarded. But might does not make right! In the face of all humanity our religious and ethical convictions demand that *every human being must be treated humanely!*

This means that every human being without distinction of age, sex, race, skin colour, physical or mental ability, language, religion, political view, or national or social origin possesses an inalienable and *untouchable dignity*. And everyone, the individual as well as the state, is therefore obliged to honour this dignity and protect it. Humans must always be the subjects of rights, must be ends, never mere means, never objects of commercialization and industrialization in economics, politics and media, in research institutes, and industrial corporations. No one stands 'above good and evil' – no human being, no social class, no influential interest group, no cartel, no police apparatus, no army, and no state. On the contrary; possessed of reason and conscience, every human is obliged to behave in a genuinely human fashion, to *do good and avoid evil!*

It is the intention of this Global Ethic to clarify what this means. In it we wish to recall irrevocable, unconditional ethical norms. These should not be bonds and chains, but helps and supports for people to find and realize once again their lives' directions, orientations, and meaning.

There is a principle which is found and has persisted in many religious and ethical traditions of humankind for thousands of years: *What you do not wish done to yourself, do not do to others!* Or in positive terms: *What you wish done to yourself, do to others!* This should be the irrevocable, unconditional norm for all areas of life, for families and communities, for races, nations and religions.

Every form of egoism should be rejected: all selfishness, whether individual or collective, whether in the form of class thinking, racism, nationalism, or sexism. We condemn these because they prevent humans from being authentically human. Self-determination and self-realization are thoroughly legitimate so long as they are not separated from human self-responsibility and global responsibility,

Non-Violence and Respect for Life

Article 5

Every person has a responsibility to **respect life.** No one has the right to injure, to torture or to kill another human person. This does not exclude the right of justified self-defence of individuals or communities.

that is, from responsibility for fellow humans and for the planet Earth.

This principle implies very concrete standards to which we humans should hold firm. From it arise *four broad, ancient guidelines* for human behaviour which are found in most of the religions of the world.

III. Four irrevocable directives

1. Commitment to a culture of non-violence and respect for life

Numberless women and men of all regions and religions strive to lead lives not determined by egoism but by commitment to their fellow humans and to the world around them. Nevertheless, all over the world we find endless hatred, envy, jealousy and violence, not only between individuals but also between social and ethnic groups, between classes, races, nations, and religions. The use of violence, drug trafficking and organized crime, often equipped with new technical possibilities, has reached global proportions. Many places are still ruled by terror 'from above'; dictators oppress their own people, and institutional violence is widespread. Even in some countries where laws exist to protect individual freedoms, prisoners are tortured, men and women are mutilated, hostages are killed.

(a) In the great ancient religious and ethical traditions of humankind we find the directive: *You shall not kill!* Or in positive terms: *Have respect for life!* Let us reflect anew on the consequences of this ancient directive: all people have a right to life, safety, and the free development of personality in so far as they do not injure the rights of others. No one has the right physically or psychically to torture, injure, much less kill, any other human being. And no people, no state, no race, no religion has the right to hate, to discriminate against, to 'cleanse', to exile, much less to liquidate a 'foreign' minority which is different in behaviour or holds different beliefs.

(b) Of course, wherever there are humans there will be conflicts. Such conflicts, however, should be resolved without violence within a framework of justice. This is true for states as well as for individuals. Persons who hold political power must work within the framework of a just order and commit themselves to the most non-

17

Article 6

Disputes between states, groups or individuals should be resolved without violence. No government should tolerate or participate in acts of genocide or terrorism, nor should it abuse women, children, or any other civilians as instruments of war. Every citizen and public official has a responsibility to act in a peaceful, non-violent way.

Article 7

Every person is infinitely precious and must be protected unconditionally. The animals and the natural environment also demand protection. All people have a responsibility to protect the air, water and soil of the earth for the sake of present inhabitants and future generations.

violent, peaceful solutions possible. And they should work for this within an international order of peace which itself has need of protection and defence against perpetrators of violence. Armament is a mistaken path; disarmament is the commandment of the times. Let no one be deceived: There is no survival for humanity without global peace!

(c) Young people must learn at home and in school that violence may not be a means of settling differences with others. Only thus can a *culture of non-violence* be created.

(d) A human person is infinitely precious and must be unconditionally protected. But likewise the *lives of animals and plants* which inhabit this planet with us deserve protection, preservation, and care. Limitless exploitation of the natural foundations of life, ruthless destruction of the biosphere, and militarization of the cosmos are all outrages. As human beings we have a special responsibility – especially with a view to future generations – for Earth and the cosmos, for the air, water, and soil. We are *all intertwined together* in this cosmos and we are all dependent on each other. Each one of us depends on the welfare of all. Therefore the dominance of humanity over nature and the cosmos must not be encouraged. Instead we must cultivate living in harmony with nature and the cosmos.

(e) To be authentically human in the spirit of our great religious and ethical traditions means that in public as well as in private life we must be concerned for others and ready to help. We must never be ruthless and brutal. Every people, every race, every religion must show tolerance and respect – indeed high appreciation – for every other. Minorities need protection and support, whether they be racial, ethnic, or religious.

2. Commitment to a culture of solidarity and a just economic order

Numberless men and women of all regions and religions strive to live their lives in solidarity with one another and to work for authentic fulfilment of their vocations. Nevertheless, all over the world we find endless hunger, deficiency, and need. Not only individuals, but especially unjust institutions and structures are responsible for these tragedies. Millions of people are without

19

Article 8

Every person has a responsibility to behave with **integrity, honesty and fairness.** No person or group should rob or arbitrarily deprive any other person or group of their property.

Article 9

All people, given the necessary tools, have a responsibility to make serious efforts to overcome poverty, malnutrition, ignorance, and inequality. They should promote sustainable development all over the world in order to assure dignity, freedom, security and justice for all people.

Article 10

All people have a responsibility to develop their talents through diligent endeavour; they should have equal access to education and to meaningful work. Everyone should lend support to the needy, the disadvantaged, the disabled and to the victims of discrimination.

work; millions are exploited by poor wages, forced to the edges of society, with their possibilities for the future destroyed. In many lands the gap between the poor and the rich, between the powerful and the powerless is immense. We live in a world in which totalitarian state socialism as well as unbridled capitalism have hollowed out and destroyed many ethical and spiritual values. A materialistic mentality breeds greed for unlimited profit and a grasping for endless plunder. These demands claim more and more of the community's resources without obliging the individual to contribute more. The cancerous social evil of corruption thrives in the developing countries and in the developed countries alike.

(a) In the great ancient religious and ethical traditions of humankind we find the directive: *You shall not steal!* Or in positive terms: *Deal honestly and fairly!* Let us reflect anew on the consequences of this ancient directive:

No one has the right to rob or dispossess in any way whatsoever any other person or the commonweal. Further, no one has the right to use her or his possessions without concern for the needs of society and Earth.

(b) Where extreme poverty reigns, helplessness and despair spread, and theft occurs again and again for the sake of survival. Where power and wealth are accumulated ruthlessly, feelings of envy, resentment, and deadly hatred and rebellion inevitably well up in the disadvantaged and marginalized. This leads to a vicious circle of violence and counter-violence. Let no one be deceived: There is no global peace without global justice!

(c) Young people must learn at home and in school that property, limited though it may be, carries with it an obligation, and that its uses should at the same time serve the common good. Only thus can a *just economic order* be built up.

(d) If the plight of the poorest billions of humans on this planet, particularly women and children, is to be improved, the world economy must be structured more justly. Individual good deeds, and assistance projects, indispensable though they be, are insufficient. The participation of all states and the authority of international organizations are needed to build just economic institutions.

A solution which can be supported by all sides must be sought for the debt crisis and the poverty of the dissolving Second World, and even more the Third World. Of course conflicts of interest are unavoidable. In the developed countries, a distinction must be made

Article 11

All property and wealth must be used responsibly in accordance with justice and for the advancement of the human race. Economic and political power must not be handled as an instrument of domination, but in the service of economic justice and of the social order.

Truthfulness and Tolerance

Article 12

Every person has a responsibility to **speak and act truthfully**. No one, however high or mighty, should speak lies. The right to privacy and to personal and professional confidentiality is to be respected. No one is obliged to tell all the truth to everyone all the time.

Article 13

No politicians, public servants, business leaders, scientists, between necessary and limitless consumption, between socially beneficial and non-beneficial uses of property, between justified and unjustified uses of natural resources, and between a profit-only and a socially beneficial and ecologically oriented market economy. Even the developing nations must search their national consciences.

Wherever those ruling threaten to repress those ruled, wherever institutions threaten persons, and wherever might oppresses right, we have an obligation to resist – whenever possible non-violently.

(e) To be authentically human in the spirit of our great religious and ethical traditions means the following:

- We must utilize economic and political power for *service to humanity* instead of misusing it in ruthless battles for domination. We must develop a spirit of compassion with those who suffer, with special care for the children, the aged, the poor, the disabled, the refugees, and the lonely.
- We must cultivate *mutual respect* and consideration, so as to reach a reasonable balance of interests, instead of thinking only of unlimited power and unavoidable competitive struggles.
- We must value a *sense of moderation and modesty* instead of an unquenchable greed for money, prestige, and consumption! In greed humans lose their 'souls', their freedom, their composure, their inner peace, and thus that which makes them human.

3. Commitment to a culture of tolerance and a life of truthfulness

Numberless women and men of all regions and religions strive to lead lives of honesty and truthfulness. Nevertheless, all over the world we find endless lies and deceit, swindling and hypocrisy, ideology and demagoguery:

- Politicians and business people who use lies as a means to success;
- Mass media which spread ideological propaganda instead of accurate reporting, misinformation instead of information, cynical commercial interest instead of loyalty to the truth;
- Scientists and researchers who give themselves over to morally questionable ideological or political programmes or to economic

writers or artists are exempt from general ethical standards, nor are physicians, lawyers and other professionals who have special duties to clients. Professional and other codes of ethics should reflect the priority of general standards such as those of truthfulness and fairness.

Article 14

The freedom of the media to inform the public and to criticize institutions of society and governmental actions, which is essential for a just society, must be used with responsibility and discretion. Freedom of the media carries a special responsibility for accurate and truthful reporting. Sensational reporting that degrades the human person or dignity must at all times be avoided.

Article 15

While religious freedom must be guaranteed, the representatives of religions have a special responsibility to avoid expressions of prejudice and acts of discrimination toward those of different beliefs. They should not incite or legitimize hatred, fanaticism and religious wars, but should foster tolerance and mutual respect between all people.

interest groups, or who justify research which violates fundamental ethical values;

- Representatives of religions who dismiss other religions as of
little value and who preach fanaticism and intolerance instead of
respect and understanding.

(a) In the great ancient religious and ethical traditions of
humankind we find the directive: *You shall not lie!* Or in positive
terms: *Speak and act truthfully!* Let us reflect anew on the consequences of this ancient directive: No woman or man, no institution,
no state or church or religious community has the right to speak lies
to other humans.

(b) This is especially true:

- For those who work in the *mass media*, to whom we entrust the
freedom to report for the sake of truth and to whom we thus
grant the office of guardian. They do not stand above morality
but have the obligation to respect human dignity, human rights,
and fundamental values. They are duty-bound to objectivity, fairness, and the preservation of human dignity. They have no right
to intrude into individuals' private spheres, to manipulate public
opinion, or to distort reality.
- For *artists, writers, and scientists*, to whom we entrust artistic
and academic freedom. They are not exempt from general ethical
standards and must serve the truth;
- For the *leaders of countries, politicians, and political parties*, to
whom we entrust our own freedoms. When they lie in the faces
of their people, when they manipulate the truth, or when they are
guilty of venality or ruthlessness in domestic or foreign affairs,
they forsake their credibility and deserve to lose their offices and
their voters. Conversely, public opinion should support those
politicians who dare to speak the truth to the people at all times.
- Finally, for *representatives of religion*. When they stir up
prejudice, hatred, and enmity towards those of different belief, or
even incite or legitimate religious wars, they deserve the condem-
nation of humankind and the loss of their adherents.

Let no one be deceived: There is no global justice without truthfulness and humaneness!

Mutual Respect and Partnership

Article 16

All men and all women have a **responsibility to show respect** to one another **and understanding** in their partnership. No one should subject another person to sexual exploitation or dependence. Rather, sexual partners should accept the responsibility of caring for each other's well-being.

(c) Young people must learn at home and in school to think, speak, and act *truthfully*. They have a right to information and education to be able to make the decisions that will form their lives. Without an ethical formation they will hardly be able to distinguish the important from the unimportant. In the daily flood of information, ethical standards will help them discern when opinions are portrayed as facts, interests veiled, tendencies exaggerated, and facts twisted.

(d) To be authentically human in the spirit of our great religious and ethical traditions means the following:

- We must not confuse freedom with arbitrariness or pluralism with indifference to *truth*.
- We must cultivate *truthfulness* in all our relationships instead of dishonesty, dissembling, and opportunism.
- We must constantly seek truth and incorruptible sincerity instead of spreading ideological or partisan half-truths.
- We must courageously *serve the truth* and we must remain *constant and trustworthy*, instead of yielding to opportunistic accommodation to life.

4. Commitment to a culture of equal rights and partnership between men and women

Numberless men and women of all regions and religions strive to live their lives in a spirit of partnership and responsible action in the areas of love, sexuality, and family. Nevertheless all over the world there are condemnable forms of patriarchy, domination of one sex over the other, exploitation of women, sexual misuse of children, and forced prostitution. Too frequently, social inequities force women and even children into prostitution as a means of survival – particularly in less developed countries.

(a) In the great ancient religious and ethical traditions of humankind we find the directive: *You shall not commit sexual immorality!* Or in positive terms: *Respect and love one another!* Let us reflect anew on the consequences of this ancient directive: No one has the right to degrade others to mere sex objects, to lead them into or hold them in sexual dependency.

Article 17

In all its cultural and religious varieties, marriage requires love, loyalty and forgiveness and should aim at guaranteeing security and mutual support.

Article 18

Sensible family planning is the responsibility of every couple. The relationship between parents and children should reflect mutual love, respect, appreciation and concern. No parents or other adults should exploit, abuse or maltreat children.

(b) We condemn sexual exploitation and sexual discrimination as one of the worst forms of human degradation. We have the duty to resist wherever the domination of one sex over the other is preached – even in the name of religious conviction; wherever sexual exploitation is tolerated, wherever prostitution is fostered or children are misused. Let no one be deceived: There is no authentic humaneness without a living together in partnership!

(c) Young people must learn at home and in school that sexuality is not a negative, destructive, or exploitative force, but creative and affirmative. Sexuality as a life-affirming shaper of community can only be effective when partners accept the responsibilities of caring for one another's happiness.

(d) The relationship between women and men should be characterized not by patronizing behaviour or exploitation, but by love, partnership, and trustworthiness. Human fulfilment is not identical with sexual pleasure. Sexuality should express and reinforce a loving relationship lived by equal partners.

Some religious traditions know the ideal of a voluntary renunciation of the full use of sexuality. Voluntary renunciation also can be an expression of identity and meaningful fulfilment.

(e) The social institution of marriage, despite all its cultural and religious variety, is characterized by love, loyalty, and permanence. It aims at and should guarantee security and mutual support to husband, wife, and child. It should secure the rights of all family members. All lands and cultures should develop economic and social relationships which will enable marriage and family life worthy of human beings, especially for older people. Children have a right of access to education. Parents should not exploit children, nor children parents. Their relationships should reflect mutual respect, appreciation, and concern.

(f) To be authentically human in the spirit of our great religious and ethical traditions means the following:

- We need mutual respect, *partnership*, and understanding, instead of patriarchal domination and degradation, which are expressions of violence and engender counter-violence.
- We need mutual concern, tolerance, readiness for reconciliation, and *love,* instead of any form of possessive lust or sexual misuse.

Only what has already been experienced in personal and familial relationships can be practised on the level of nations and religions.

29

Conclusion

Article 19

Nothing in this Declaration may be interpreted as implying
for any state, group or person any right to engage in any
activity or to perform any act aimed at the destruction of

IV. A transformation of consciousness

Historical experience demonstrates the following: Earth cannot be changed for the better unless we achieve a transformation in the consciousness of individuals and in public life. The possibilities for transformation have already been glimpsed in areas such as war and peace, economy, and ecology, where in recent decades fundamental changes have taken place. This transformation must also be achieved in the area of ethics and values! Every individual has intrinsic dignity and inalienable rights, and each also has an inescapable responsibility for what she or he does and does not do. All our decisions and deeds, even our omissions and failures, have consequences.

Keeping this sense of responsibility alive, deepening it and passing it on to future generations, is the special task of religions. We are realistic about what we have achieved in this consensus, and so we urge that the following be observed.

1. A universal consensus on *many disputed ethical questions* (from bio- and sexual ethics through mass media and scientific ethics to economic and political ethics) will be difficult to attain. Nevertheless, even for many controversial questions, suitable solutions should be attainable in the spirit of the fundamental principles we have jointly developed here.

2. In many areas of life a new consciousness of ethical responsibility has already arisen. Therefore we would be pleased if as many *professions* as possible, such as those of physicians, scientists, business people, journalists, and politicians would develop up-to-date codes of ethics which would provide specific guidelines for the vexing questions of these particular professions.

3. Above all, we urge the various *communities of faith* to formulate their very *specific ethic*: what does each faith tradition have to say, for example, about the meaning of life and death, the enduring of suffering and the forgiveness of guilt, about selfless sacrifice and the necessity of renunciation, about compassion and joy? These will deepen, and make more specific, the already discernible global ethic.

In conclusion, we appeal to all the inhabitants of this planet. Earth cannot be changed for the better unless the consciousness of individuals is changed. We pledge to work for such transformation in individual and collective consciousness, for the awakening of our spiritual powers through reflection, meditation, prayer, or positive any of the responsibilities, rights and freedom set forth in this Declaration and in the Universal Declaration of Human Rights of 1948.

The proposed Universal Declaration of Human Responsibilities has the endorsement of the following individuals:

I. The InterAction Council Members

Helmut Schmidt (Honorary Chairman), Former Chancellor of the Federal Republic of Germany
Malcolm Fraser (Chairman), Former Prime Minister of Australia

Andries A. M. van Agt, Former Prime Minister of the Netherlands
Anand Panyarachun, Former Prime Minister of Thailand
Oscar Arias Sánchez, Former President of Costa Rica
Lord Callaghan of Cardiff, Former Prime Minister of the United Kingdom
Jimmy Carter, Former President of the United States
Miguel de Ia Madrid Hurtado, Former President of Mexico
Kurt Furgler, Former President of Switzerland
Valéry Giscard d'Estaing, Former President of France
Felipe González Márquez, Former Prime Minister of Spain
Mikhail Gorbachev, Former State President of the USSR
Kenneth Kaunda, Former President of Zambia
Lee Kuan Yew, Former Prime Minister of Singapore
Kiichi Miyazawa, Former Prime Minister of Japan
Misael Pastrana Borrero, Former President of Colombia (died in August 1997)
Shimon Peres, Former Prime Minister of Israel
Maria de Lourdes Pintasilgo, Former Prime Minister of Portugal
José Sarney, Former President of Brazil
Shin Hyon Hwad, Former Prime Minister of the Republic of Korea
Kalevi Sorsa, Former Prime Minister of Finland

thinking, for a *conversion of the heart*. Together we can move mountains! Without a willingness to take risks and a readiness to sacrifice there can be no fundamental change in our situation! Therefore we commit ourselves to a common global ethic, to better mutual understanding, as well as to socially-beneficial, peace-fostering, and Earth-friendly ways of life.

> *We invite all men and women,*
> *whether religious or not,*
> *to do the same.*

This was subscribed to by:

Bahai: Juana Conrad – Jacqueline Delahunt – Dr Wilma Ellis – Charles Nolley – R. Leilani Smith – Yael Wurmfeld.
Brahma Kumaris: B.K. Jagdish Chander Hassija – B.K. Dadi Prakashmani.
Buddhism: Rev. Koshin Ogui, Sensei. **Mahayana:** Rev. Chung Ok Lee. **Theravada:** Dr A.T. Ariyaratne – Preah Maha Ghosananda – Ajahn Phra Maha Surasak Jivanando – Dr Chatsumarn Kabilsingh – Luang Poh Panyananda – Ven. Achahn Dr Chuen Phangcham – Ven. Dr Havanpola Ratanasara – Ven. Dr Mapalagama Wipulasara Maha Thero. **Vajrayana:** His Highness the Fourteenth Dalai Lama. **Zen:** Prof. Masao Abe – Zen Master Seung Sahn – Rev.Samu Sunim.
Christianity: Blouke Carus – Dr Yvonne Delk. **Anglican:** Rev. Marcus Braybrooke – James Parks Morton. **Orthodox:** Maria Svolos Gebhard. **Protestant:** Dr Thelma Adair – Martti Ahtisaari – Rev. Wesley Ariarajah – Dr Gerald O. Barney – Dr Nelvia M. Brady – Dr David Breed – Rev. John Buchanan – Bishop R. Sheldon Duecker – Prof. Diana L. Eck – Dr Leon D. Finney, Jr – Dr James A. Forbes, Jr – Bishop Frederick C. James – Archbishop Mikko Juva – Prof. James Nelson – Dr David Ramage, Jr – Robert Reneker – Rev. Dr Synginan Rhee – Rev. Margaret Orr Thornas – Prof. Carl Friedrich von Weizsäcker – Prof. Henry Wilson – Rev. Addie Wyatt. **Roman Catholic:** Rev. Thomas A. Baima – Cardinal Joseph Bernardin – Fr Pierre-François de Béthune – Sister Joan M. Chatfield MM – Rev. Theodore M. Hesburgh CSC – Abbot Timothy Kelly OSB – Jim Kenney – Prof. Hans Küng – Dolores Leakey – Sister Joan Monica McGuire OP – Rev. Maximilian Mizzi – Dr Robert Muller – Rev. Albert Nambiaparambil – Bishop Placido Rodriguez – Bishop Willy Romélius – Dorothy Savage – Brother David Steindi-Rast OSB – Brother Wayne Teasdale.

Pierre Elliott Trudeau, Former Prime Minister of Canada
Ola Ullsten, Former Prime Minister of Sweden
George Vassiliou, Former President of Cyprus
Franz Vranitzky, Former President of Austria

II. Experts

(Preparatory meetings in Vienna, Austria in March 1996 and April 1997 and special guests at the 15th Plenary Session in Noordwijk, The Netherlands, in June 1997)

Hans Küng (academic advisor to the project), Tübingen University
Thomas Axworthy (academic advisor to the project), CRB Foundation
Kim, Kyong-dong (academic advisor to the project), Seoul National University

Cardinal Franz König, Vienna, Austria
Anna-Marie Aagaard, World Council of Churches
M. Shanti Aram , World Conference on Religion and Peace and member of the Indian Parliament (died June 1997)
A.T. Ariyaratne, President of the Sarvodaya Movement of Sri Lanka
Julia Ching, University of Toronto
Hassan Hanafi, University of Cairo
Nagaharu Hayabusa, Asahi Shimbun, Tokyo
Kim Yersu, Director of the Division of Philosophy and Ethics, UNESCO
Peter Landesmann, Member of the European Academy of Sciences, Salzburg
Lee, Seung-yun, Former Deputy Prime Minister and Minister of Economic Planning, Republic of Korea
Flora Lewis, journalist of the *International Herald Tribune,* Paris
Liu, Xiao-feng, Institute of Sino-Christian Studies, Hong Kong
Teri McLuhan, Canadian author
Isamu Miyazaki, Former State Minister, Economic Planning Agency of Japan, Tokyo
James Ottley, Anglican observer at the United Nations, New York
Richard Rorty, Stanford Humanities Center
L.M. Singvi, High Commissioner for India, London
Seiken Sugiura, House of Representatives of Japan, Tokyo

Native religions: His Imperishable Glory Bambi Baaba. **Akuapi:** Nana Apeadu. **Yoruba:** His Royal Highness Oseijeman Adefunmi I – Baba Metahochi Kofi Zannu. **Native American:** Archie Mosay – Burton Pretty on Top – Peter V. Catches.

Hinduism: Dr M. Aram – Jayashree Athavale-Taiwarkar – His Highness Swami Chidananda Saraswafi – Swami Chidananda Saraswafi Muniji – Swami Dayananda Saraswafi – Sadguru Sant Keshavadas – P. V. Krishnayya – Dr Lakshmi Kumari-Amrish Mahajan – Dr Krishna Reddy – Prof. V. Madhusudan Reddy – Swami Satchidananda – His Highness Satguru Sivaya Subramuniyaswami – His Highness Dr Bala Siva Yogindra Maharaj. **Vedanta:** Pravrajika Amalaprana – lrravrajika Prabuddhaprana – Pravnajika Vivekaprana.

Jainism: Dr Raslnnikant~Gardi. **Digambar:** Narendra P. Jain. **Shwetambar:** His Highness Shri Atmanandji – Dipchand S. Gardi – His Excellence Dr L. M. Singhvi – His Highness Acharya Sushil Kumarji Maharaj.

Judaism: Helen Spector – Sir Sigmund Sternberg. **Conservative:** Professor Susannah Heschel. **Reform:** Rabbi Herbert Bronstein – Norma U. Levitt – Rabbi A. James Rudin – Rabbi Herman Schaalman – Dr Howard A. Sulkin. **Orthodox:** Prof. Ephraim Isaac.

Islam: Tan Sri Dato' Seri Ahmad Sarji bin Abdul-Hamid – Dr Qazi Ashfaq Ahmed – Hamid Ahmed – Mazar Ahmed – Hon. Louis Farrakhan – Dr Hamid Abdul Hai – Mohammed A. Hai – Dr Mohammad Hamidullah – Dr Aziza al-Hibri – Dr Asad Husain – Dato Dr Haji Ismail bin Ibrahim – Dr Irfan Ahinat Kilan – Qadir H. Khan – Dr Abdel Rahman Osman. **Shi'ite:** Prof. Seyyed Hossein Nasr. **Sunni:** Imam Dawud Assad – Imam Warith Deen Mohammed – Hon. Syed Shahabuddin.

Neo-pagans: Rev. Baroness Cara-Marguerite-Drusilla – Rev. Deborah Ann Light – Lady Olivia Robertson.

Sikhs: Sin Singh Sahbi Bhai Sahib Harabhajan Singh Khalsa Yogiji – Bhai Mohinder Singh – Dr Mehervan Singh – Hardial Singh – lndarjit Singh – Singh Sahib Jathedar Manjit Singh – Dr Baiwant Singh Hansra.

Taoists: Chungliang Al Huang.

Theosophists: Radha Burnier.

Zoroastrians: Dastoor Dr Kersey Antia – Dr Homi Dhalla – Dastoor Dr Kaikhusroo Minocher JamaspAsa – Dastoor Jehangir Oshidari – Rohinton Rivetna – Homi Taleyarkhan – Dastoor Kobad Zarolit-Dastoor Mehraban Zarthosty.

Inter-religious organizations: Karl Berzolheimer – Dr Daniel Gómez-Ibáñez – Ma Jaya Bhagavati – Peter Laurence – Dr Karan Singh – John B. Taylor – Rev. Robert Traer – Dr William F. Vendley.

Koji Watanabe, Former Japanese Ambassador to Russia
Woo, Seong-yong, Munhwa Ilbo, Seoul
Alexander Yakovlev, Former Member, Presidential Council of
the Soviet Union

III. Supporters

Lester Brown, President, Worldwatch Institute
André Chouraqui, Professor in Israel
John B. Cobb Jr, Claremont, California, USA
Takako Doi, President, Japan Socialist Democratic Party
Ekaterina Genieva, Member of the State Duma, Moscow
Marjorie Hewitt Suchocki, Dean, School of Theology,
Claremont, California, USA
Henry A.Kissinger, Former Secretary of State, USA
Teddy Kollek, Former Mayor of Jerusalem
William Laughlin, American entrepreneur
H. H. Chwasan Lee Kwang Jung, Won Buddhism, Korea
Dmitry S.Lichatchov, literary historian, Academy of Sciences,
St Petersburg
Rabbi Professor J. Magonet, Principal of the Leo Baeck
College
Robert S. McNamara, Former President, World Bank
Konrad Raiser, General Secretary of the World Council of
Churches, Geneva
Chief Rabbi Jonathan Sacks, London
Sir Sigmund Sternberg, OStJ KCSG JP, Three Faiths Forum,
London
Paul Volcker, Chairman, James D. Wolfensohn Inc.
Carl Friedrich von Weizsäcker, Starnberg

IV. Sponsors

Shinyasu Hoshino, President, National Institute for Research
Advancement, Tokyo
Ayako Sono, Chairperson, Nippon Foundation, Tokyo
Kim Woo-Joong, Chairman, Dae-Woo Corporation, Seoul

Part One: The Declaration of the Parliament of World Religions

Introduction

HANS KÜNG

Today, no one can still have any serious doubts that a period of the world which has been shaped more than any before it by world politics, world technology, the world economy and world civilization, needs a world ethic. That means a **fundamental consensus concerning** binding values, irrevocable standards, and personal attitudes. Without a basic consensus over ethics any society is threatened sooner or later by chaos or a dictatorship. There can be no better global order without a global ethic.

Here a global ethic means neither a global ideology, nor a single unified global religion transcending all existing religions, nor a mixture of all religions. Humanity is weary of unified ideologies, and in any case the religions of the world are so different in their views of faith and 'dogmas', their symbols and rites, that a 'unification' of them would be meaningless, a distasteful syncretistic cocktail.

Nor does a global ethic seek to replace the high ethics of the individual religions with an ethical minimalism. The Torah of the Jews, the Christians' Sermon on the Mount, the Muslims' Qur'an, the Hindus' Bhagavadgita, the Discourses of the Buddha, the Sayings of Confucius – for hundreds and millions of men and women all these remain the foundation for faith and life, thought and action. What then?

A global ethic seeks to work out what is already common to the religions of the world now despite all their differences over human conduct, moral values and basic moral convictions. In other words, a global ethic does not reduce the religions to an ethical minimalism but represents the minimum of what the religions of **the world already have in common now in the ethical sphere**. It is not directed against anyone, but invites all, believers and non-believers, to make this ethic their own and act in accordance with it.

For the first time in the history of religions, the Council of the Parliament of the World's Religions, which met in Chicago from 28 August to 4 September 1993, and in which 6,500 people from every possible religion took part, ventured to work out and present a 'Declaration Toward a Global Ethic'. As was only to be expected, this declaration provoked vigorous discussion during the Parliament. However, the welcome thing is that at a time when so many religions are entangled in political conflicts, indeed in bloody wars, representatives of very different religions, great and small, endorsed this Declaration with their signatures on behalf of countless believers on this earth.

This Declaration now forms the basis for an extensive process of discussion and acceptance which we hope will be sparked off in all religions. For of course this Declaration Toward a Global Ethic – like the first Declaration on Human Rights in 1776 at the time of the American Revolution – is not an end but a beginning. That was clear from the start, and it was expressed clearly again at the end of the Parliament when this declaration was termed an 'Initial Declaration Toward a Global Ethic'. The hope is that this document may set off a process which changes the behaviour of men and women in the religions in the direction of understanding, respect and cooperation. And if all goes well, in the not too distant future we shall have other declarations which make the global ethic of the religions more precise and concrete and add further illustrations to it. Perhaps one day there may even be a United Nations Declaration on a Global Ethic to provide moral support for the Declaration on Human Rights, which is so often ignored and cruelly violated.

But is not such an expectation sheer illusion? Can the religions be expected to accept such a declaration? Are such hopes realistic? To the eternal sceptics and pessimists we would say: No one will deny that within the space of two or three decades it has proved possible to bring about world-wide a universal change of awareness about economics and ecology, about world peace and disarmament, and about the partnership between men and women. Our document here has been written and approved in the hope that a similar change of awareness may take place over a basic ethic common to all humankind, a global ethic. It is up to the religions of this earth and to people all over the world, in a quite practical way, wherever they are, to make sure that this Declaration remains more than paper, that it is filled with life, that it inspires people to a life of mutual respect, understanding and co-operation.

The History, Significance and Method of the Declaration Toward a Global Ethic

HANS KÜNG

It was a historic week, the week from 28 August to 4 September 1993, during which the delegates of the Parliament of the World's Religions discussed the Declaration Toward a Global Ethic and then – the vast majority of them – signed it. The beginning of that week had brought the sensational news that Israel and the Palestine Liberation Organization (PLO) had agreed on a peace plan. In concrete terms that meant mutual recognition by the two arch-enemies and limited autonomy for parts of the occupied Palestinian territories. All at once prospects for a lasting peace in the Middle East had increased considerably. But this was a peace towards which the religions and their representatives – the representatives of Judaism, Islam and Christianity – should have made a greater contribution than they had done previously, by each opposing the fundamentalists in its own ranks. For there can be no peace among the nations without peace among the religions!

However, in that same week the peace negotiations between the Orthodox Serbs, the Catholic Croats and the Muslim Bosnians had collapsed again. And there is no doubt that the religions which are also involved here had neglected in the period of more than forty years since the Second World War to engage in mourning, honestly confess the crimes which had been committed by all sides in the course of the centuries, and ask one another for mutual forgiveness. Similarly, there is no doubt that the Catholic and Orthodox churches in particular have identified themselves all too much with their own political leadership in the most recent controversies and not made a commitment for peace openly, opportunely and energetically. Again I think that there can be no peace among the nations without peace among the religions! Still, I found it significant that the Finnish negotiator in Geneva for peace in Bosnia-Herzegovina, the diplomat Martti Ahtisaari, as I was told, had in his hands not only the draft plan for peace in this region but also the Declaration of the Parliament of the World's Religions Toward a Global Ethic and signed it immediately as the right word at the right time. And I have no doubt that the President of the International Committee of the Red Cross in Geneva, Dr Cornelio Sommaruga, would also have put his personal signature to this declaration, which incorporates so many principles of the International Red Cross, had he not been prevented in principle from signing any such declarations because of the need for his high office to be neutral. For there can be no human survival without a common human ethic, a global ethic!

The Red Cross, which grew out of a small 'Committee' around Henri Dumant and is therefore still called the 'Committee of the Red Cross' today, is perhaps the most hopeful example of how quite a small group can stand at the origins of a great initiative which initially does not seem very hopeful, yet in the end can have world-wide influence. The Declaration Toward a Global Ethic also goes back to the bold initiative of a very small group: I want to tell its story briefly here.

45

1. The prehistory

Since 1989 I had been in contact with the local group which was interested in a centenary celebration of the First Parliament of World Religions in Chicago in September 1993.

From 7 to 10 February 1989 a colloquium had taken place at UNESCO in Paris for which I wrote the basic paper; I was also able to suggest the names of people to respond to it. It was entitled 'Pas de paix entre les nations sans paix entre les religions', and the respondents, all professors, were Masao Abe (Kyoto) for Buddhism, Mohammed Arkoun (Paris) for Islam, Eugene B. Borowitz (New York) for Judaism, Claude Geffré (Paris) for Christianity, Liu Shu-hsien (Hong Kong) for Chinese religion, Bithika Mukerji (Benares) for Hinduism and Karl-Josef Partsch (Bonn) from the perspective of international law.

On 9–10 March 1989 I gave similar lectures at the universities of Toronto and Chicago: 'No peace among the nations without peace among the religions'. In the lecture in the Rockefeller Chapel of the University of Chicago I called on those responsible for planning the centenary celebration of the 1893 World Parliament of Religions to proclaim a century later a 'new ethical consensus' of the religions. However, it was all still very unclear at that time, apart from two things. First, the second Parliament should not be left to a certain religious sect with considerable financial resources which had already shown interest in it. And secondly, the Divinity School of the University of Chicago – where I had been visiting professor in the winter semester of 1981 and had had rich scholarly inter-religious experiences – did not want to involve itself in the matter as such. However, on my return to Tübingen I received an invitation dated 28 April 1989 from the then Administrator of the Council for a Parliament of the World's Religions, Ron Kidd, with whom I had spoken, to draft the first outline of a declaration on a common ethic for the Parliament in collaboration with a team in Chicago. I agreed in principle, but the plans for the trip to Chicago that was needed and a planned meeting in Washington on the occasion of a later lecture did not work out.[1]

My book *Global Responsibility* appeared in German in 1990. All my experiences with the problems of a global ethic, above all at UNESCO and also at the World Economic Forum in Davos, had come together in this book, and in it I could already discuss in breadth the need for a global ethic in the context of the world religions and the world economy. The next year an English-American edition had also appeared under the title *Global Responsibility. In Search of a New World Ethic.* The preface to this edition had been written by Prince Philip, Duke of Edinburgh – to whom I remain most deeply grateful – who remarked that in this book there was a discussion of 'what is probably the most critical and challenging issue in the debate about the future of the human habitation of this globe'.

A pragmatic American, Professor Swidler of the Religion Department of Temple University, Philadelphia, and editor of the *Journal of Ecumenical Studies,* then composed an appeal in which among other things he called for the prompt composition of a declaration on a global ethic. Having become somewhat sceptical after my experiences with numerous actions and appeals of this kind, I personally responded at first in a somewhat restrained way, but in the end decided to become the first signatory to Swidler's appeal, after making some corrections. I also sought out some signatories in Europe. The key sentences from this appeal run: 'Such efforts should concentrate on drawing together the research and reflection on Global Ethic and related matters into a "Universal Declaration of a Global Ethos" which would then be circulated to the various forums of all the religions and ethical groups for appropriate revisions – with a view to eventual adoption by all the religions and ethical groups of the world. Such a "Universal Declaration of a World Ethic" could then serve a function similar to the 1948 "Universal Declaration of Human Rights" of the United Nations – a kind of standard that all will be expected to live up to ... The "Universal Declaration of a Global Ethos" would in a major way bring to bear the moral and spiritual resources of all the religions and ethical groups on the basic ethical problems of the world, which are not easily susceptible to political force.' So this appeal was finally published and was signed by important theologians and scholars in religious studies.[2] I myself had the opportunity to present the declaration in connection with a further lecture to the UNESCO authorities in Paris and to discuss it with representatives of both Judaism and Islam, Rabbi René Samuel Sirat, President of the Permanent Council of the Conference of European Rabbis, and Tadjini Haddam, Rector of the Muslim Institute of the Great Mosque of Paris.

In the meantime of course *Global Responsibility* had also been read in Chicago, and on 27 February 1992 the 'Council' for the preparation of the World Parliament finally sent its Executive Director, Dr Daniel Gómez-Ibáñez, to Tübingen. His task was to persuade me definitively to undertake the draft of a Declaration by the Parliament on a Global Ethic, which I was to write in Tübingen. People in Chicago envisaged a document of two to three pages. However, it was clear to me that things could not be done this way if the aim was to provide more than a casual 'poster'. Of course a well-argued declaration could not be written in a few days or weeks. So when despite other burdens I finally promised to write a 'Declaration' for a 'Global Ethic' (not vaguely for 'Global Values', which was originally proposed by Chicago), I did so in awareness of the fact that the Parliament of the World's Religions provided a quite unique opportunity for the concern for a global ethic. It was important to seize it.

2. The preparations for the text

I now devoted my teaching programme for the summer semester of 1992 completely to this theme. Instead of having a seminar on postmodernity, I held an inter-disciplinary and inter-religious colloquium on 'Human Rights – World Religions – World Ethic'. This time, too, I was able to rely on the friendship of Tübingen colleagues, the Indologist Heinrich von Stietencron and the Islamist Josef van Ess, with whom I had already given dialogue lectures on *Christianity and the World Religions* (which were published in 1984). Along with the Sinologist Professor Karl-Heinz Pohl they helped me to find competent dialogue partners from the other religions for this colloquium. At the same time they made a substantial contribution towards clarifying the fundamental questions of principle by their own scholarly contributions.

During our colloquium the responses by distinguished representatives of the other religions were important for me: the contribution by the Chinese professor Li Zehou, living in exile, and the leading Thai Buddhist and social reformer Sulak Sivaraska, along with those of Rabbi Dr David Krochmalnik, the Hindu Dr Vasudha Dalmia, the Muslim Dr Roswitha Badry, and the Austrian Buddhist Alois Payer. Furthermore Dr Heiner Bielefeldt, an expert on human rights questions, helped us to examine the ethical potential of the 1948 United Nations Declaration of Human Rights and the 1949 Basic Law of the Federal Republic of Germany and to provide precise criteria for distinguishing between law and ethic, rights and ethics.

Nevertheless, at the end of the summer semester of 1992 I continued to be unclear how such a declaration should be structured and put into words. And everything depended on structure and style. The structure had to be clear (not over-complex) and the style totally comprehensible (no technical language). What should be the guidelines for such a declaration? The classical virtues? From the start that seemed to me rather boring. Or particular problem areas, which was the special wish of my students from our Institute, who with the utmost commitment represented the younger generations? But this seemed to me to be simply too difficult in view of the complex problem areas of sexual and marital morality, the ethics of the economy, the media and the state.

As a first stage I had simply drafted a **preamble** and not only given it to our colloquium but at the beginning of June 1992 also sent it to several competent scholars in different world religions. I had built up my own **small consultative network,** which comprised correspondents from Europe to America, from Central Africa to Bangladesh. I also canvassed the idea at lectures throughout the world – those at the World Conference of Religions for Peace in Mainz, the World Congress of Faiths in London, the International Association for Religious Freedom in Hamburg, the Shalom Hartman Institute in Jerusalem, the World Economic Forum in Davos, the Temple of Understanding and the United Nations in New York were particularly important – and had countless discussions with believers of very different religions (and of course also with 'non-believers'). In particular I am most grateful for suggestions from the former Deputy General Secretary of the United Nations and Chancellor of the UNO Peace University in Costa Rica, Dr Robert Muller; the physicist and philosopher Carl-Friedrich von Weizsäcker of Starnberg; and the educational specialist Professor Reijo E. Heinonen of Turku, Finland, along with reactions from scholars in religion like Professor Julia Ching of Toronto, Professor Ursula King of Bristol and Professor Peter Antes of Hanover, not to forget Professor Johannes Lähnemann of Erlangen, an expert in religious education, who organized a Congress on 'Global Ethic and Education' in Nuremberg in autumn 1994.

On 14 July 1992 the **first draft** of the Universal Declaration was ready and was immediately sent to the experts for comments and corrections. Without exception it met with great approval; its basic structure remained unchanged, but it was considerably improved by numerous detailed suggestions. On 12 October 1992 the **second improved draft** was ready and on 23 October 1992, to my great relief, I could send the English translation prepared by Professor Leonard Swidler to Chicago in the hope that I would have corrections from there by the beginning of 1993, so that I could produce the definitive text.

However, there was now an unexpectedly long pause. My draft was discussed in the 'Council' in Chicago and made available to all the members of the Board of Trustees. Further experts were brought in and the discussion circle was extended.[3] Finally, various cardinals and bishops attentively studied the draft, as did scholars and monks of non-Christian religions. It was only on 13 June 1993 (in the middle of a summer semester now burdened with quite a different set of problems) that I finally received an answer from Dr Daniel Gómez-Ibáñez to the draft which I had sent in October 1992. But it was pleasantly positive: it called for improvements to the English translation and contained various suggestions for corrections to content and style, and also the short form of the Declaration that was desired.

Supported as always by my colleague Dr Karl-Josef Kuschel, who was to accompany me to the Parliament of the World's Religions, as best I could I incorporated all the corrections (along with others which had arrived in the meantime) and thus on 17 July 1993 – after further translation by Professor Swidler – was thus able to send the **definitive English text** to Chicago. There it underwent only further minor corrections and was approved by the Board of Trustees. The initial basic structure and language had remained the same through all the phases, but details of the text had been considerably improved. More than a hundred people from all the great religions had been involved in the process of consultation.

Unfortunately, however, it was now no longer possible, as had originally been planned, to present the Declaration to some internationally known representatives of the great religions for examination and acceptance. The prior endorsement of religious and spiritual personalities would doubtless have eased the acceptance of the Declaration in the Parliament of the World's Religions and in public. Nor was the text of the Declaration immediately sent to all the members of the Parliament, as had previously been agreed, but only to the roughly 200 'delegates' of the various religions, and finally also – with an embargo which was soon broken – to the press. Finally, the text was discussed in the assembly of the delegates. I shall report on that in due course.

First, though, let us turn to the questions of hermeneutics and method which had to be considered in connection with a declaration on a global ethic.

3. What had to be avoided in a declaration on a global ethic

I readily acknowledge that for a long time I was quite perplexed as to what the content and style of such a declaration should be. On the one hand there were no historical models: for the first time in the history of the religions a declaration on an ethic was to be worked out which was to be acceptable to the adherents of all religions. But on the other hand for a long time I did not have the necessary intuition of the declaration as a whole, the perspective from which it should be written and the kind of language it should use. For the declaration that was envisaged had to be all of a piece, with no dry paragraph work, no colourful bouquet of quotations, no academic discourse, no diplomatic communiqué, none of those compromise products which usually emerge from committee work. 'The world has never been redeemed by a committee', John Courtney Murray once remarked to me during the Second Vatican Council. He was a pioneer American Catholic in a new democratic understanding of church and state, and author of the draft of the famous Declaration of the Second Vatican Council on Religious Liberty. Since then this sentence has been stamped on my mind. It was clear to me that though a declaration on a global ethic of course could not do without the 'input' of a great many heads, it needed a concept and a programme for developing the material.

In fact even the many inter-disciplinary discussions which I have reported, with their countless suggestions on points of detail, could not simply 'produce' an overall conception. But as a result of them, in succession I gained three essential insights.

1. It was indispensable – against the background of today's world – to make a clear distinction between the ethical level and the purely legal or political level and at the same time to give a precise definition of the term 'global ethic' (Part I).
2. The fundamental ethical demand on all men and women and all human societies or institutions should be a basic principle the beginnings of which one finds in every great religious or ethical tradition: 'Every human being must be treated humanely.' There was also the 'Golden Rule', which can similarly be demonstrated in all the great traditions: 'Do not do to another what you would not want to be done to you!' (Part II[4]).
3. These fundamental ethical demands can be made concrete in four ancient directives which can also be found in all the great religions: 'Do not kill, do not steal, do not lie, do not commit sexual immorality' (Part III[5]).

In a friendly private meeting after the penultimate session of the colloquium on 2 July 1992, with my colleagues Li Zehou, Sulak Sivaraksa, Heinrich von Stietencron and Karl Heinz

Pohl, it dawned on me what should be done about the third and most different concrete part, and that it could be shaped by those four ancient directives. But of course that had not yet answered the question how all this was to be done. There were various negative and positive criteria to be noted which had come home to me in the course of discussion.

First of all, negatively: what was the declaration on a global ethic **not** to be? To put it schematically:

(a) **No reduplication of the Declaration of Human Rights**. If religions essentially only repeated statements from the UN Declaration of Human Rights, one could do without such a declaration; however, an ethic is more than rights. And certainly such a declaration on an ethic would not escape the charge made especially by the Indian religions, that this was a typically 'Western' document.

However, a declaration on a global ethic should provide ethical support for the UN Declaration of Human Rights, which is so often ignored, violated and evaded. Treaties, laws, agreements are observed only if there is an underlying ethical will really to observe them.

(b) **No political declaration**: if religions made concrete statements on questions which were directly related to world politics or economics like the Middle East conflict or the resolution of the debt crisis, the difference between the political and the ethical levels would not be observed and the declaration on a global ethic would immediately be drawn into the maelstrom of world-political discussions and confrontations; it would deepen the political dissent rather than bridge it. So no specific modern Western theory of the state or society can form the basis of such a declaration.

However, a declaration on a global ethic should also have relevance at the economic and political levels and support efforts towards a just ordering of the economy and of society.

(c) **No casuistic moral sermon.** If religions only admonished with a raised finger or a threatening fist; got lost in a flood of commandments and precepts, canons and paragraphs; indeed wanted to make binding statements on every possible difficult case (even in so popular an area as sexual ethics), they would be a priori rejected by many people today and certainly not be able to produce a consensus. To enter into moral questions like divorce or euthanasia which are disputed in all religions and nations would be to torpedo such a declaration from the start.

However, a declaration on a global ethic should not hesitate to make clear statements even about uncomfortable truths and demands – like respect for all life – and should not leave out the sexual sphere.

(d) **No philosophical treatise.** If religions relied on a modern philosophical ethics, whether inspired more by analytic linguistic philosophy, Frankfurt Critical Theory, or a theory of history, they would presumably hardly get beyond problematical generalizations and pragmatic models (with transcendental, utilitarian or even regional bases). However, a declaration on a global ethic should address more than intellectuals or educated people.

Still, a declaration on a global ethic should readily take up all the stimuli provided by philosophy and should be formulated in such a way that philosophers – and indeed also agnostics and atheists – could accept it, even if they did not share the transcendent ground of such a declaration.

(e) **No enthusiastic religious proclamation.** If religions simply invoke cosmic consciousness, global harmony, spiritual creativity, universal unity, all-embracing love and a spiritual vision of a better world, or hymn mother earth and in so doing do not take sufficiently seriously the economic, political and social reality of today's highly complex industrial society, they are alienating themselves from reality, as far as

55

both the world and they themselves are concerned. On the other hand a consensus of religions on a particular anthropology (e.g. the relationship of body and soul) or a particular metaphysics (e.g. the relationship of space, time and supreme being or self) is not to be expected and therefore is not to be expressed in a declaration on a global ethic.

However, a declaration of the religions on a global ethic should clearly indicate that it is a declaration by men and women with a religious motivation who are convinced that the present empirical world is not the ultimate, supreme, 'absolute' spiritual reality and truth.

4. What a declaration on a global ethic should contain

Along with these negative demarcations came some positive pointers, which I shall now list. In positive terms, what should a declaration on a global ethic contain? Programmatically, such a declaration must penetrate to a deeper ethical level, the level of **binding values, irrevocable criteria and inner basic attitudes,** and not remain stuck at the legal level of laws, codified rights and paragraphs with which issue might be taken, or at the political level of proposing concrete political solutions. Despite all its consequences for specific areas, an ethic is primarily concerned with the inner realm of a person, the sphere of the conscience, of the 'heart', which is not directly exposed to sanctions that can be imposed by political power (the power of the state, the courts, the police); – must be capable of **securing a consensus:** moral unanimity and not just numerical unanimity is to be striven for. So statements should be avoided which are a priori rejected by one of the great religions. Condemnations which are understood as a violation of religious feelings are counterproductive;

– must be **self-critical:** the declaration should not just be addressed to the 'world', but also and primarily to the religions themselves. Their frequent failure, particularly in making peace, should not be concealed, but be stated unequivocally. To this degree such a declaration must have the character not only of gentle confirmation but of constructive provocation;

– must be **related to reality**. From beginning to end the world must be seen as it really is and not just as it should be. So the starting point must always be what is, with a progression from there to what should be. To recognize the real significance of norms which initially seem general it is necessary to begin with certain negative experiences. What is truly human is not always easy to divine, but anyone can give a few examples of what is really inhuman;

– must be **generally comprehensible**: technical arguments and scientific jargon, of whatever origin, are to be avoided. Everything must be expressed in a language which at least the ordinary newspaper reader can understand and which can also be translated into other languages. It is not rationalism to avoid irrational statements; it is not irrationalism to remain open to the super-rational ('beyond the limits of pure reason');

– must have a **religious foundation**: even if all men and women are to be addressed, including those who are not religious, it should be made plain that for religions, an ethic has a religious foundation. For those with a religious motivation, an ethic has to do with trust (quite rational trust) in an ultimate supreme reality, whatever name this may be given and no matter what the dispute over its nature may be among the different religions.

The declaration should have the name 'Declaration Toward a Global Ethic', not 'Global Ethics'. 'Ethic' means a basic human moral attitude, whereas 'ethics' denotes the philosophical or theological theory of moral attitudes, values and norms. Unfortunately, it is not as easy to make this distinction in all languages as it is in German, as I already noted in connection with the translations of my book *Projekt Weltethos,* which in English became *Global Responsibility.* Thus the Greek word 'ethos' is not used much in most languages, and even the term 'world' cannot be combined with 'ethos' or 'ethic' in a word as it can be in German, where we talk quite naturally of world history, world politics, world economy, world society, using a single word. The result of the discussion with translators and publishers was that the following terms would be used for the German 'Weltethos':

- in English 'world ethic' or 'global ethic' (not 'ethics', which like the German word 'Ethik' means the doctrine or the system),
- in French 'éthique planétaire',
- in Spanish 'ética mundial',
- in Italian, 'etica mondiale',
- in Czech 'svetový étós', and so on.

However, the choice of word is not ultimately decisive here. It is the subject-matter, not the name, which is important. Anyone who even in German prefers for whatever reason to speak of global, universal or planetary ethics can of course do so. These terms refer to the same thing. However, 'Weltethos' has already become established as 'global ethic'.

Still, particularly in view of the religious character of the declaration, from the beginning the difficult question now arises: should such a declaration be promulgated as it were in the name of God? To Christians, Jews and Muslims that seems a matter of course, but it is not.

5. In the name of God? The Buddhists' objection

If all religions were to be involved in a declaration on a global ethic and at least no important ones were to be excluded, then one would have to dispense with naming God: this was clear to me from the beginning, reluctant though I was to accept it as a Christian theologian. 'In the name of God, the

58

almighty, creator of heaven and earth': certainly it would have been easier to argue in this way in respect of unconditionally valid norms. But in that case one would have to have left out **Buddhism**, one of the great world religions. It was clear to me from the start that the representatives of Buddhism would not have accepted the name of God in such a declaration. And moreover there was immediately a controversy over this even during the Parliament. So I want to explain this point in more detail.

Buddhism – a **religion without God**? Of course experts in Buddhism can point out that Buddhism as practised **in reality** does know 'God', indeed a number of gods taken over from popular religion (Indian religion or some others): those personified natural forces or divinized kings and saints who are called on for protection and help (there are phenomena corresponding to such practical polytheism in popular Catholicism with its veneration of saints and angels). The Buddha Gautama himself regarded the gods *(devas)* as real but provisional, since they too were subject to birth and rebirth.

On the other hand, for Buddhists divine beings have a form of being far beyond human beings. So for the Buddha, who always regards himself as a human being and not a god, it is quite consistent to gain the help of the gods for this-worldly matters not related to redemption (rain, the blessing of children – just as in Christianity heavenly helpers, angels and archangels standing near to God are often invoked for help). In short, in Buddhism there are gods, and these are to be venerated, as numerous passages in the Pali canon commend. So in the sphere of Buddhism we do not find a strict atheism but a polytheism – often crudely magical. However, the gods are not 'Ultimate Reality', absolute 'Ground' and 'Primal Goal'. So there *was* need for caution in a common invocation of the name of God in a declaration on a global ethic.

For of course Christians, and with them Jews and Muslims – the three religions of a Semitic Near Eastern origin and prophetic character – do not mean by the name of God one god among many, not even the highest, but the one and only God, Creator and Perfecter of the world and human beings. And of course in this understanding, 'God' is the 'last and first reality'. But Buddhism sees God against an Indian horizon: he is like the Indian god Brahman,who is proudly enthroned on the pyramid of gods and is similarly subject to coming to be and passing away. As for a personal creator God, Buddha Gautama already confessed his ignorance and his indifference: completely intent on redeeming human beings from suffering, he rejects answers to speculative questions like those about God and the origin of the world. In this sense, on this higher level, Buddhism is, if not atheistic, at least resolutely agnostic.

Now a rational **dialogue** about this basic difference, too, is quite **possible** between the monotheistic prophetic religions and the different branches of Buddhism (Theravada, Mahayana and Vajrayana). It is a dialogue which has to concentrate on the comparison of the concept of God with the basic Buddhist concepts of Nirvana, Shunyata and Dharmakaya. These are all terrns which the great majority of Buddhists do not understand in a nihilistic way but as a positive reality, and which can be regarded by Christians as parallel terms for the Absolute. They fulfil analogous functions to the concept of God. At an earlier stage, when as a theologian I was naturally interested not only in the ethical but also and primarily in 'dogmatic questions' (of faith), I tried to describe how for a deeper Jewish-Christian-Muslim understanding of God (as the last/first, highest/deepest reality) God himself is all this in one:

– 'Nirvana', in so far as he is the goal of the way of redemption;

- 'Shunyata' (void), in so far as he continually escapes all affirmative definitions;
- 'Dharmakaya' (body of teaching), in so far as law governs the cosmos and human beings;
- 'Adi Buddha' (primal Buddha), in so far as he is the origin of all.[6]

But these brief remarks show clearly enough that here we come up against an extremely difficult problem, and that we did well to avoid naming the name of God in our Declaration Toward a Global Ethic. The reaction of Buddhists during the Parliament confirmed this. For because some religious leaders of the various guest committees, with the best intentions in the world, had quite ingenuously used the names 'God the Almighty' and 'God the Creator' in their invocations, prayers and blessings at the opening plenary and on other occasions, and had spoken of the need to 'strive for a unity of religions under God', **leading Buddhists during the Parliament felt called on to protest.**

At the beginning of the first session of the 'Assembly' of the religious leaders, the Ven. Samu Sunim of the Zen Buddhist Temple in Chicago read out a statement[7] in which he complained of the lack of knowledge and sensitivity on the part of certain religious leaders: 'With great astonishment we watched leaders of different traditions define all religions as religions of God and unwittingly rank Buddha with God.' And because this had happened, the Buddhists now wanted to state: 'We would like to make it known to all that Shakyamuni (Gautama) Buddha, the founder of Buddhism, was not God or a god. He was a human being who attained full Enlightenment through meditation and showed us the path of spiritual awakening and freedom. Therefore, Buddhism is not a religion of God. Buddhism is a religion of wisdom, enlightenment and compassion. Like the worshippers of God who believe that salvation is available to all through confession of sin and a life of prayer, we Buddhists believe that salvation and enlightenment is available to all through removal of defilements and delusion and a life of meditation. However, unlike those who believe in God who is separate from us, Buddhists believe that Buddha which means 'one who is awake and enlightened' is inherent in us all as Buddhanature or Buddhamind.'

However, this statement by the Buddhists was by no means limited to criticism. Apart from the invitation to take seriously the different approaches of the religions to spirituality and salvation as a prerequisite for a Parliament of the World's Religions, two of their concerns seem to me to be particularly welcome:

– The **affirmation of concern for a global ethic**: 'We feel that we the religious leaders of the world gathered here at this historic Parliament of the World's Religions must establish strong guidelines for religious tolerance and cooperation and serve as inspirations for the different religious communities in the world.'

– The **concern for language and communication**: 'We must train ourselves to be sensitive to each other and learn to use language which is inclusive and all-embracing. We suggest we use "Great Being" or "Power of the Transcendent" or "Higher Spiritual Authority" instead of God in reference to the ultimate spiritual reality. We are open to other suggestions and discussions on this matter.'

This abundantly confirms what I have already said myself about a deeper understanding of God in the light of the Buddhist tradition.

6. Disputed questions

The Buddhist objections to the use of the name of God, which were heard by the delegates in respectful silence, were already evidence that a consensus can be achieved in matters relating to a global ethic only if, as I suggested in my *Global*

Responsibility, one leaves aside all differences of faith and 'dogma', symbols and rites, and concentrates on common guidelines for human conduct. That is true not only in connection with dogmatic demands by Christians but also in connection with the demands from the sphere of the Indian religions (which are often no less dogrnatic), when these for example presuppose a universality of ideas (for example about consciousness and supreme being) which does not in fact exist, or even assert a unity of spintual experience and thus of the religions. In so doing they sometimes neglect all the divisive differences among the religions, something which is only possible on the basis of a pantheistic or mystical view of unity (Brahman Atman), which is not even capable of commanding a consensus.

Of course there were further discussions within the framework of the 'Assembly' of religious leaders. But these were to relate above all to the future of the Parliament of Religions and questions about collaboration. The Declaration itself had already gone through a process of wide inter-religious consultation and had been accepted. Given the complexity of the problems and the limitations of time it was hardly possible to hold an effective discussion, and so no discussion in the Parliament had originally been provided for (the 1990 Seoul Church Assembly had been a warning to us!). All that had been sought had been a free testimony to the assent of all participants (and not just the 'delegates') who wanted to sign – on the basis of their insight into the text, the consultation that had taken place, and the authority of the first internationally known signatories who had originally attached their names to the Declaration.

However, this was not what happened. Contrary to the original agreement, the 'Council' had held back the Declaration Toward a Global Ethic so as to be able to present it at the end as an effective conclusion – not least with the media in view. It had been supplied to the 'Assembly', but with the proviso that now they could only discuss it, and could not make any changes. But that led to objections (understandable in some, but not all respects) from those who rejected the procedure itself (which had not been explained at all to the delegates) and encouraged those who had problems with individual points of content. By far the majority of critics had no idea of the broad process of inter-religious consultation which had been connected with the composition of the Declaration.

Furthermore, because of the situation I have described, the 'Assembly' discussed not only the Declaration Toward a Global Ethic but also practical and political questions. In particular, representatives of the native Indian population of America and Black Americans used this assembly to propose verbal motions, presented on the spot, in support of their concerns (which are all too justified), without there being time to discuss these seriously. The lack of an agenda made it difficult for the Chairperson of the Assembly, Dr David Ramage, to bring order to a debate which often became passionate. Finally, in view of the various motions, he decided that the 'Assembly', which had no legislative competence, had to refrain from voting on any resolutions whatsoever.

As far as the Declaration Toward a Global Ethic was concerned, the proposal of a Muslim to demote it to a working paper did not secure a majority. Since the discussion of the Declaration took place at the first session of the 'Assembly' at separate round tables, it was not easy to discover where the objections lay. But three points seem to have played a part.

(a) In the section on the culture of **non-violence** some people – particularly in view of the desperate situation of the Muslims in Bosnia – felt that the **right to self-defence** (which is also affirmed by the United Nations Charter) was not brought out clearly enough. To that, of course, it can be replied that the Declaration deliberately took a middle course which could secure a consensus: between a 'Realpolitik' of force in resolving conflicts and an unrealistic unconditional pacifism which, confronted with violence, expulsion, rape, death and mass murder, unconditionally repudiates the use of force. First of all the Declaration states in principle: 'Such conflicts, however, should be resolved without violence within a framework of justice. This is true for states as well as for individuals.' However, it immediately adds: 'Persons who hold political power must work within the framework of a just order and commit themselves to the most non-violent, peaceful solutions possible. And they should work for this within an international order of peace which itself has need of protection and defence against perpetrators of violence' (III 1 b). And in connection with the legal and economic order it is stated: 'Wherever those ruling threaten to repress those ruled, wherever institutions threaten persons, and wherever might oppresses right, we are obligated to resist – whenever possible non-violently' (III 2 d).

It follows from this that the right to self-defence is clearly affirmed both for the individual and for the collective – but in the context of a culture of non-violence it applies only *in extremis*, in extreme instances, namely when non-violent resistance is senseless. In the face of brutality, barbarism and genocide, self-defence is said to be permissible. No further holocaust of any people whatever can simply be accepted in a pacifist way. On the other hand, no simple formula of legitimation for military intervention of any kind is to be offered: no 'just wars' in the service of interests which are all too clearly economic, political and military are to be justified in this way.

(b) Of course the objections to the culture of equal rights and the partnership of man and woman, made more in an underhand way than openly, also had to be taken seriously. It was claimed that the text of the Declaration said too little about the family; this could easily be refuted, given the statements about marriage, family and nurture, parents and children, but was provoked by the English translation which at some points had rendered the German 'in the family' with 'at home'.

However, it must be conceded that what is said in this section about **equal rights for women** doubtless presents a challenge not only to some Muslims and Hindus but also to more conservative European and American Christians. Certainly the Declaration deliberately says nothing about the role of women in worship; the ordination of women to the priesthood is a highly controversial question in most Christian churches and does not belong in any consensus document. But even without such a statement there are individual statements in this section about women which must prompt certain Christians, Muslims and Hindus to reflect on their own positions.

It should be remembered that now we cannot just repeat ancient directives from our Holy Scriptures, including those relating to women, in a sterile way, but have to translate them into present-day terms. Not least as a result of Dostoievsky's perceptive legend of the Grand Inquisitor, Christians have become accustomed to asking: 'What would he (the Messiah Jesus) say if he were to come again?' Could not the analogous question be equally meaningful for Muslims: 'What would he (the Prophet Muhammad) say if he were to come again?' Presumably both Jesus and Muhammad would have a good deal to say, particularly on the question of women.

(c) The objection had been expressed from one particular side that the whole Declaration was **'too Western'**. The objection did not go into detail, but the purport was probably that in this Declaration everything had not been reduced to key-words like 'cosmic consciousness', 'global spiritual harmony', 'bond with the universe', 'unity of soul and cosmos'. However, it must be conceded that of course a declaration will differ, depending on whether it has been drafted by a Thai monk, an Indian Swami, a Japanese Zen master, a Jewish Rabbi, a Muslim Ayatollah or a Christian theologian. Each has his own approach, his own style, and brings with it his own basic cultural and religious colouring. I had always been aware of my own religious and cultural relativity; but the process of inter-religious and international consultation at the beginning was meant to make this relativity as tolerable as possible. In the declaration I had two concerns.

– Nothing was to be included which could not expect to find a consensus. And a 'cosmic consciousness of unity' presents considerable problems, even in India among Hindus, Sikhs and Muslims. Certainly the cosmos and responsibility for it is constantly present in our Declaration, but 'cosmic consciousness', 'unity of the soul and the universe' could not be generic spiritual nouns in a declaration to which religions of non-Indian origin had to assent.

– In this declaration it was necessary to think through what could be said in common by the great religious traditions for the present situation. Certainly things that were quite incapable of commanding a consensus had to be avoided, but at the same time the consequences of particular ethical maxims had to be expressed clearly and made concrete, even if this was inconvenient for certain religious communities.

The emergence of criticism inside and outside the 'Assembly' was important when one sensed how the individual religious communities were beginning to come to terms with this text intensively. But at the same time it must be said that the controversy was not really at the centre. I was quite delighted to note three things in particular in this discussion.

– No side put in question the need for a Declaration Toward a Global Ethic and its usefulness.

– The basic ethical requirement that 'Every human being must be treated humanely' was accepted as a matter of course (furthermore, it also found a way into the experts' draft of a UNESCO Declaration on Tolerance in Istanbul in April 1993).

– The second complementary basic demand, the Golden Rule, was similarly accepted as a matter of course.

In the draft of the Declaration, from beginning to end I had avoided any quotations of sacred texts: had I not done so there would have been no end to the quotations, because this or that group would have called for a further quotation as a witness from its own tradition on this point or that. But the **Golden Rule** in particular, which is so fundamental, shows impressively that the **common global ethic** of the religions is **not a new invention** but **only a new discovery**. Here again I would like to cite some formulations of the Golden Rule.

– Confucius (*c.*551–489 BCE): 'What you yourself do not want, do not do to another person' (Sayings 15.23).

– Rabbi Hillel (60 BCE to 10 CE): 'Do not do to others what you would not want them to do to you' (Shabbat 31a).

– Jesus of Nazareth: 'Whatever you want people to do to you, do also to them' (Matt. 7.12; Luke 6.31).

– Islam: 'None of you is a believer as long as he does not wish his brother what he wishes himself' (Forty Hadith of an-Nawawi, 13).

– Jainism: 'Human beings should be indifferent to worldly things and treat all creatures in the world as they would want to be treated themselves' (Sutrakritanga I, 11, 33).

– Buddhism: 'A state which is not pleasant or enjoyable for me will also not be so for him; and how can I impose on another a state which is not pleasant or enjoyable for me?' (Samyutta Nikaya V, 353.3–342.2).

– Hinduism: 'One should not behave towards others in a way which is unpleasant for oneself: that is the essence of morality' (Mahabharata XIII 114, 8).

That brings us to the perspectives for the future.

7. A sign of hope

That such a declaration – and the quality of the signatures should be noted – should in the end have been signed by such significant people as the Dalai Lama and the Cardinal of Chicago, the Vatican representative and the representative of the World Council of Churches, the General Secretary of the World Conference of Religions for Peace and the General Administrator of the International Baha'i Community, the spiritual head of the Sikhs in Amritsar and a president of the Lutheran World Alliance, the patriarch of Cambodian Buddhism, a leading rabbi and an Arab sheikh, represents an unmistakable sign of hope for the future of religions and the peace of the world which beyond question could hardly have been expected only a short time ago.

It will now be an enjoyable task for the scholars of the various religions to work out the project for a global ethic further in the light of their own religions and to bring out three things:
– how strongly the Declaration Toward a Global Ethic is rooted in their own tradition;
– how far their own tradition corresponds with other ethical traditions;
– how far their own tradition has a distinctive, specific, special contribution to make to the ethic.

It need not be repeated that this global ethic should not and cannot strive to be a world ideology or a unitary world religion beyond all existing religions, nor a mixture of all religions. Similarly I should make it clear that even in the future, the global ethic cannot replace, say, the Torah of the Jews, the Christian Sermon on the Mount, the Muslim Qur'an, the Hindu Bhagavadgita, the Discourses of Buddha or the Sayings of Confucius. How could anyone come to think that the different religions wanted to avoid the foundation for their faith and life, thought and actions? These sacred scriptures offer as it were a maximal ethic, compared with which the Declaration Toward a Global Ethic can offer only a minimal ethic. But that does not of course mean an ethical minimalism, though it would already be a great gain if only this minimum of common values, criteria and basic attitudes were realized. What I mean is the minimum of what is now already common to the ethic of the religions of the world and which hopefully can be extended and deepened in the course of the process of communication.

However, the question of a common global ethic is not concerned only with a problem between religions. **Society as a whole is challenged** at a time when after the murder of a two-year-old child by two ten-year-olds now even news magazines like *Der Spiegel* lament in their headlines a crisis of orientation, indeed an '**orientation jungle**' and a removal of tabus without precedent in the history of culture: 'The youngest generation must cope with a confusion of values the extent of which it is difficult to estimate. It can hardly recognize clear criteria for right and wrong, good and evil, of the kind that were still being communicated in the 1950s and 1960s by parents and schools, churches and sometimes even politicians.'[8]

And the editor of the greatest German weekly, *Die Zeit*, Theo Sommer, after the many scandals in politics, business and the trade unions, also appeals to the conscience of the intellectuals: 'The intellectuals of our country must also quite certainly examine themselves. Many of them have preached self-fulfilment to excess; they have mocked virtue, respectability and style; they have for a while taken postmodern arbitrariness so far that in accordance with the slogan 'Everything goes', nothing is taboo any more. The criteria are dissolving in the corrosive acid bath of criticism.'[9]

This crisis of orientation is certainly a problem not only for Europe but also for America, and especially also for the area of the former Soviet Union and for China; in other words, it is a global problem.

Are there prospects of a realization of this Declaration? Of course no one knows. It is clear that 'global ethic' has now become a programmatic term and that now a great many people acknowledge particular common principles of a global ethic. But it is also certain that the Declaration Toward a Global Ethic is not yet the realization of a global ethic. Such a declaration cannot be an end; it can only be the means to an end. And what comes of it will depend on everyone, on you and me.

However, a decisive start has been made. Who in our generation must not concede that he or she did not think as much thirty years ago about nature and the preservation of the natural foundations of life, peace and disarmament, the partnership of men and women, as they do today? A change of global consciousness has taken place in humanity in these three spheres and is constantly expanding. Why should not the same be true of a common ethic for humankind? Surely in thirty years people will think quite differently again about the need for a common ethic for humankind? It should be granted to the younger generation in all the religions on earth, who could then have more orientation, more courage to live and certainly also more true joy in life.

Notes

1. Together with the Protestant theologian Jürgen Moltmann I was preparing an issue of the international theological journal *Concilium* for April 1990 devoted to the topic *The Ethics of World Religions and Human Rights,* which was meant to help to clarify the theoretical theme.

2. Muhammed Arkoun (Muslim), Julia Ching (Confucian/Catholic), John Cobb (Methodist), Khalid Duran (Muslim), Heinrich Fries (Catholic), Claude Geffré (Catholic), Irving Greenberg (Jewish), Norbert Greinacher (Catholic), Riffat Hassan (Muslim), Rivka Horwitz (Jewish), John Hick (Presbyterian), Gerfried Hunold (Catholic), Adel Khoury (Catholic), Paul Knitter (Catholic), Karl-Josef Kuschel (Catholic), Pinchas Lapide (Jewish), Johannes Lähnemann (Protestant), Dietmar Mieth (Catholic), Paul Mojzes (Methodist), Jürgen Moltmann (Protestant), Fathi Osman (Muslim), Raimon Panikkar (Hindu/Buddhist/Catholic), Daniel Polish (Jewish), Rodolfo Stavenhagen (sociologist), Theo Sundermeier (Protestant), Tu Wei-Ming (Confucian). Cf. *Journal of Ecumenical Studies* 28.1, editorial, and *Süddeutsche Zeitung*, 16/17 November 1991.

3. The main participants in the discussions in Chicago were Jeffrey Carlson (De Paul University), Manford Vogel (NorthWestern University), Robert Marshall (Lutheran School of Theology at Chicago = LSTC), Yoshiro Ishida (LSTC), Ilona Klemens (LSTC), James A. Scherer (LSTC), Ron Kidd (Institute for World Spirituality), David Breed (CPWR), Kyaw Than (LSTC), Tanveer Azmat (Islamic Research Foundation), Infan Ahmad Khan (American Islamic College), John Kaserow (Catholic Theological Union), William Schweiker (University of Chicago, Divinity School), Charles Strain (De Paul University), Mary R. Garrison (De Paul University). Also consulted were Professor David Tracy (University of Chicago, Divinity School), Professor Robert Schreiter (Catholic Theological Union), Rabbi Herman Schaalman, Dr Ghulam Haider Aasi, Dr Chuen Phangcham, Dr Richard Luecke, the Ecumenical Officer of the Archdiocese of Chicago, Thomas Baima, along with many others.

4. I had long reflected on the fundamental ethical demand for truly human behaviour. Cf. H. Küng, *On Being a Christian* (1974), London and New York 1976, D II.1, 'Norms of the Human'; id., *Does God Exist? An Answer for Today* (1978), London and New York 1980, chapters E II 3, 'Fundamental Trust as the Basis for Ethics'; F IV 4, 'Consequences for Ethics: Theologically Justified Autonomy'. This book also shows that this approach has little to do with the 'natural theology' which is feared above all by Protestant theologians of the Barthian school.

5. Here I could take up the beginnings of my *Global Responsibility* (Chapter A VI, 'Ethical Perspectives of the World Religions').

6. For these difficult problems see H. Küng (with J. von Ess, H. von Stietencron and H. Bechert), *Christianity and the World Religions. An Introduction to Dialogue with Islam, Hinduism and Buddhism* (1984), New York and London 1986, Chapter C III 2: 'Buddhism – atheistic?'

7. The statement was also signed by the supreme patriarch of Cambodian Buddhism, Ven. Maha Chosananda, by Zen Master Seung Sahn, by the Ven. Abbot Walpola Piyananda (Sri Lanka Buddhism), the Rev. Chung Ok Lee (Korean Buddhism) and the Thai professor Chatsumarn Kabilsingh.

8. *Der Spiegel* no. 9 , 1993.

9. *Die Zeit,* leading article of 21 May 1993.

Part Two: A Universal Declaration of Human Responsibilities by the InterAction Council

Introduction

HELMUT SCHMIDT

It is natural that after the end of a dictatorship a nation should set about guaranteeing basic rights – in the language of the United Nations, 'human rights' – as one of its most urgent tasks. Similarly, too, after the simultaneous end of Hitler's dictatorship in Europe and the Japanese military dictatorship in East and South-East Asia, the 1948 United Nations Declaration of Human Rights was a natural, necessary and good decision.

The creation of a democratic constitution goes hand in hand with the establishing of the fundamental rights of the individual. That is what happened, thank God, after Mussolini and Hitler, and that is what happened in the Eastern half of Europe after the end of the Communist dictatorships. By contrast, the experience of the last decades unfortunately also shows that democracy and human rights can remain no more than paper pledges if a government persists merely in professing them, and both in everyday life and particularly in emergencies neglects to stand up for human rights and to make sure that they actually function. Conversely, some people are under the misapprehension that their personal freedom means being able to exercise and implement their rights – and their claims – without any personal responsibility. But if everyone pursues his or her own rights exclusively and does not accept any kind of obligations and responsibilities, a people and a state – or humankind as a whole – can deteriorate into hostilities, conflicts and finally chaos.

Keeping rights and responsibilities in balance

Without a sense of responsibility on the part of individuals, freedom can deteriorate into the domination of the strong and the powerful. Therefore it is a constant task of politicians and citizens to keep rights and responsibilities in balance.

Today, almost half a century after the Universal Declaration of Human Rights, the necessary moral imperative of that declaration to humankind and its two hundred sovereign states is in danger. First, the term 'human rights' is being used by some Western politicians, especially in the USA, as a battle cry and as an aggressive instrument for exerting pressure in foreign policy. This usually happens quite selectively: against China, Iran or Libya, but not against Saudi Arabia, Israel or Nigeria. The reason for such one-sidedness lies in economic and strategic interests.

Secondly, human rights are regarded by some Muslims, Hindus and Confucians as a typically Western concept and are sometimes even denounced as an instrument for extending Western domination. Furthermore, particularly in Asia we hear the accusation, which must taken seriously and for which there are serious reasons, that the concept of basic rights neglects or even fails to recognize the need for virtues and for obligations and responsibilities on the part of the individual towards the family, the community, society or the state. Some Asians think that they can recognize a opposition in principle between the Western and the Asian views of human dignity.

Certainly there is no disputing the fact that images of being human and the notion of human dignity differ within any society or culture – depending on the religious or philosophical or ideological standpoint. However, as a rule there are in fact great differences between the prevalent notions in Europe and North America on the one hand and the Islamic, Hindu, Buddhist and Confucian notions prevalent in Asia on the other – not to mention Communism in its several forms.

It is therefore conceivable that a 'clash of civilizations' of the kind outlined by Samuel Huntington could come about in the twenty-first century. The explosion of the world population – a fourfold increase! – in the twentieth century and its increasing concentration in great urban masses will continue at least deep into the coming century; therefore – despite the end of the bipolar conflict between the Soviet Union and the West – there will also be conflicts of power in the twenty-first century. We may hope that they will be resolved more smoothly than they were in the twentieth century. But we must fear that they could issue in a struggle between civilizations which in principle and indeed at a deep level are hostile to one another. Here fundamentalists on both sides, who from a global perspective are in most cases playing only minority outsider roles today, could possibly become the catalysts and instigators of mass hysteria. The present-day extension and intensification of an economic alliance which spans the world, known as globalization, would by no means necessarily oppose this, especially as it will involve conflicts of economic interest in novel forms.

Since the end of the Soviet block and above all since the opening up of China, the number of people involved in the competition in the open world economy has now already doubled. In addition there has been an enormous technological leap – above all in the fields of telecommunications, air transport and sea container transport – and a historical high-point in the liberalization of trade, above all in the movement of money and capital. At the beginning of the new century, almost all over the world the nations and their national economies will depend on one another to a greater degree than in any previous generation. But at the same time this globalization is leading to new, hitherto unknown rivalry. Attempts to use power politics to cheat for one's own advantage in this world competition will grow.

If in the face of this danger the nations and their states, the politicians and similarly the guardians and preservers of the religions, do not learn to respect one another's religious and cultural heritage and one another's civilizations, and if people do not learn to keep in balance the two categorical imperatives of freedom and responsibility, then indeed peace between them could collapse. The structure of world politics and the social and economic well-being of the nations may well be deeply damaged.

An interreligious, international draft

Therefore at the end of the old century – fifty years after the Universal Declaration of Human Rights, it is high time to talk similarly about human responsibilities. A minimum of ethical standards recognized all over the world is urgently necessary for intercontinental coexistence – not only for individual conduct but also for political authorities, for religious communities and churches, and for nations. And it is necessary not just for governments, but also for companies engaged in international production, trade or finance. These companies are now in danger of succumbing to a new, unrestricted, world-wide speculative robber capitalism. The need to be aware of one's own responsibility also applies to the electronic media which are active internationally; these run the risk of poisoning people all over the world with an excess of accounts of murders, shootings, acts of violence and abuse of all kinds.

The need to avoid a 'clash of civilizations' has led a large number of elder statesmen (former state presidents and heads of governments) from all five continents to present the draft of a Universal Declaration of Human Responsibilities. It is based on years of preliminary work by religious, philosophical and political leaders from all over the world and from all the great religions. The task is first to prompt a discussion;

the hope is finally to arrive at a similar UN Declaration to that of 1948, when on the initiative of Eleanor Roosevelt the United Nations approved the Universal Declaration of Human Rights.

Like the Declaration of Human Rights at that time, the additional Declaration of Responsibilities would have the character of an ethical appeal, not the binding character of international law. However, in the meantime regional packages of human rights have been created on the moral foundation of the Declaration of Human Rights which do have the binding character of international law, for example the European Convention on Human Rights and the establishment of the European Court of Human Rights. We might also recall here the great influence of the Final Helsinki Declaration and its 'Basket III' on the internal development of European Communism. Comparably, at a later stage legal or political effects from the Declaration of Responsibilities are to be hoped for.

Those who regard the authors and signatories of the draft of a Universal Declaration of Human Responsibilities as mere idealists who do not have their feet on the ground have neither an adequate historical view of the actual historical influence of the Declaration of Human Rights, which initially was not legally binding in any way, nor an adequate notion of the dangers to humankind in the future; they could simply be conservative supporters of what is wrongly called *Realpolitik*, which in principle has no morals.

Our draft repeats in Article 4 the 'Golden Rule' which plays an important role in all world religions (and which in a refined formulation Immanuel Kant elevated to become the 'categorical imperative'): 'What you do not wish to be done to yourself, do not do to others.' Article 9 states: 'All people have a responsibility ... to overcome poverty, malnutrition, ignorance, and inequality. They should promote sustainable development all over the world in order to assure dignity, freedom, security and justice for all people.' Article 15 says that the representatives of the religions have the responsibility to avoid expressions of prejudice and acts of discrimination towards those of other beliefs, but should foster tolerance and mutual respect between all people. Finally, Article 19 states that nothing in this declaration may be interpreted as implying any right aimed at the destruction of the responsibilities, rights and freedom set forth in the Declaration of Human Rights of 1948.

The need for Germany to catch up

Among us in Germany, too, today rights are rated more highly than obligations. Claims are often put forward in an excessively loud voice, while in many spheres of our society the responsibility of every individual is hardly taught and therefore hardly perceived either. Many politicians, many business executives, do not meet their obligations, nor do many universities or television channels. A largely permissive education is orientated all too one-sidedly on basic rights, and there is virtually no mention of basic obligations. Heedless egotistical 'personal fulfilment' appears as an ideal, while the common good is an empty phrase.

The second main section of the Weimar constitution bore the programmatic heading 'Basic Rights and Basic Responsibilities of Germans'; it directly related the rights of citizens to their responsibilities. An echo of this still remains in some of the individual state constitutions in force today, but there is nothing of it in the Basic Law. In Article 163 the Weimar constitution even spoke of a 'moral obligation' to work. Today some business executives cannot recognize any moral obligation to create jobs and places in training schemes. They increasingly follow the ideology of shareholder value and replace moral obligations with share prices and dividends. And conversely, some people who have no job find that they can get by on their state benefit plus a bit of moonlighting; for them this is at any rate more convenient and therefore preferable to the burden of a regular working week.

Hans Jonas with his 'imperative of responsibility', Marion Countess Dönhoff with the call to 'civilize capitalism', and Amitai Etzioni with his communitarian call for a 'responsible society' have for the moment remained very solitary voices in Germany. But without cultivating civic virtues, our society will degenerate into a politicizing wrangle between interested parties. Certainly many years ago the German constitutional experts were concerned with the question of the constitutional dimension of basic obligations within the framework of our Basic Law: however, their discussions at the time did not have any recognizable effect. By contrast, as early as 1948, in Article 29 the UN Declaration of Human Rights at least made the quite general statement that 'everyone has duties to the community in which alone the free and full development of his personality is possible'.

Our society needs education to an awareness of ethical obligations and personal responsibility. That does not mean that we have to expand our laws or even our Basic Law to this end. But our schools and colleges, our churches, our political parties, our businesses and trade unions, must recognize that the pursuit of rights without a real sense of responsibility can lead to chaos. Yet a consciousness of responsibility presupposes that we know our obligations; therefore general education towards a readiness for criticism must include the critical capacity to recognize one's own obligations. The old Roman principle *salus publica suprema lex*, public well-being is the supreme law, remains a good orientation here.

In the West, the discussion of the draft of a Universal Declaration of Human Responsibilities will prompt at least two main objections. First, practitioners of so-called *Realpolitik* will say that it is idealistic, and has no prospect of being generally accepted or put into practice. Secondly, committed champions of human rights will say that if the draft Declaration of Human Responsibilities is regarded as a twin or a pendant to the Declaration of Human Rights, there is a danger that human rights will be transposed to the level of mere morality. By contrast, in Asia some will say that while the draft meets essential principles of Asian cultural traditions and is therefore to be welcomed, its explicit attachment to the Declaration of Human Rights is superfluous, detrimental and therefore to be rejected.

Mahatma Gandhi listed seven 'social sins'. At their head stand 'politics without principles' and 'commerce without morality'. Who would contradict that? In a discussion of the Draft Declaration of Human Responsibilities the *Financial Times* recently wrote: 'Correct: we need universal rules for good business practice ... It would benefit everyone if a Universal Declaration of Business Responsibilities percolated through to the brains of company directors.' This approach, too, could become fruitful if in fact the draft Declaration of Human Responsibilities sparked off a world-wide discussion. At any rate it will be discussed in the United Nations and therefore by governments.

In addition, a public discussion would contribute to our once again reminding ourselves of the basic insight that we citizens have not only rights to defend ourselves against the despotism of others, but also obligations and responsibilities towards our fellow human beings. No democracy and no open society can survive in the long run without the twofold principle of rights and responsibilities.

The nations, states and their governments involved in economic globalization must work together towards a minimal ethical code; otherwise the new century could prove as full of conflict as the century which is now coming to an end. But this time the conflicts would not remain limited to parts of continents; there could in fact be a world-wide conflict between different basic convictions in which the parties involved would appeal to religious and cultural interpretations handed down to them. Those who want to avoid the clash of civilizations which threatens need not only economic and military potential but a morality which can be recognized by everyone else.

From the Declaration of the Religions to the Declaration of the Statesmen

Stages in the Composition of the Declaration on Human Responsibilities

JOHANNES FRÜHBAUER

Countless people from all over the world, individuals and commissions, took part directly or indirectly in producing the draft text of a 'Universal Declaration of Human Responsibilities'.[1] Stimuli, suggestions and advice about problems of language and content and improvements of the draft once it had been made came from many sides. However, the many-sided international involvement should not conceal a decisive fact: as so often in great enterprises, the initiative began with a small group, and in the end only a few people proved to be the motive force behind the whole project. The work and involvement of individuals cannot therefore be over-estimated. And finally, the InterAction Council provided the impulse: it initiated the process of discussion and institutionalized it in its ranks. So before looking at the complex process and the decisive stages of the origin of the Declaration of Human Responsibilities a brief description needs to be given of some of the basic features of the InterAction Council.

1. The InterAction Council in Rome (1987)

The InterAction Council was founded in 1983 by Takeo Fukuda (1905–1995; Prime Minister of Japan 1976–79) as a loose association of former heads of state and of government.[2] His **basic idea** was to mobilize the experience, influence and international contacts of individuals who had occupied the highest offices of state in their countries. The members of the InterAction Council, who at that time numbered around thirty, make it their prime task to develop analyses of political, economic and social problems with which humankind finds itself confronted, above all in global contexts, and to recommend solutions.

The prime **aim** is the **encouragement and improvement of international collaboration** in three main areas:

- Peace and security,
- the revival of the global economy,
- development, population and environment.

Starting from these wide groups of themes, the InterAction Council chooses specific problems and develops **concrete proposals for action**. These are then communicated directly to heads of government and other national decision-makers and to the leading figures in international organizations and influential personalities. Since its foundation in 1983, so far fifteen annual meetings of the body have taken place in various parts of the world. Each time, as a concluding document a statement has been approved which contains a series of concrete proposals on the topic which has been discussed. The **topics** have extended from questions of arms control, through the problem of unemployment and the debt question, to questions of the environment and energy.

For the first time in recent history, in 1987 leading political figures met with religious and intellectual leaders to exchange knowledge and experience and in this way to make a contribution to the well-being of humankind. The place for

85

the dialogue was the headquarters in Rome of **La Civiltà Cattolica**, the earliest Italian professional journal (founded 1850). The journal is edited by Jesuits and its contributions present the broad spectrum of the humane sciences. All the continents were represented by women and men from politics, and in addition by religious and intellectual leaders from most of the great religions of the world: Buddhism, Hinduism, Judaism, Christianity and Islam.[3] In the preface to the statement approved in La Civiltà Cattolica, the founder of the InterAction Council, Takeo Fukuda, indicated the aim of the discussion forum and thus already presented the perspective for the further programme of the InterAction Council: 'I have long felt that world peace and the welfare of mankind concern religious groups as much as political figure. I felt that an understanding could be obtained from religious groups and that a certain common denominator might be found.'[4]

World peace, the world economy and development, population and the environment were the group of themes which stood at the centre of the meeting and which were also the themes of the closing statement. Central comments from the Statement on Global Questions[5] are:

- First, the contacts made at La Civiltà Cattolica must be continued by the InterAction Council and other organizations.
- Secondly, the ethical principles which the participants share lead to the final conclusion that a true peace can be achieved only by an ongoing process of dialogue and mutual understanding which permeates all spheres of society and international relationships.
- Thirdly, for moral, political and economic reasons humankind must strive for a balanced economic structure which can remove world-wide poverty: moreover there is an enormous need to encourage a sense of world-wide solidarity with a view to survival.

- Fourthly, on the issue of development, population and the environment the significance of the mutual responsibility of women and men for family planning is emphasized and an accelerated implementation of hitherto positive experiences is called for.

According to Fukuda in his preface the agreement between politicians and religious figures aimed at in Rome was an encouragement to pursue this course. But although the InterAction Council in its annual sessions took up and developed various of the individual themes of the Rome meeting, almost a decade passed until this course that had begun was then in fact continued – in a very concrete way. In the meantime, however, elsewhere and quite independently, what had been thought about and addressed in Rome had been developed programmatically, reflected on systematically, and finally put into the form of a comprehensive declaration.

II. *Global Responsibility* (1990) and the Chicago Parliament of the World's Religions (1993)

The two basic notions which Hans Küng presented systematically and comprehensively in his book *Global Responsibility*[6] show, first, that a peace among the nations is impossible without peace among the religions, and, secondly, that despite all the dogmatic differences, a certain ethical consensus can already be found now among the religions of this world. In other words, what is shared in the ethics of the religions can form the basis for a global ethic: a minimal **basic consensus** in respect of binding values, irrevocable criteria and basic moral attitudes. This basic consensus can be supported and followed by both believers and non-believers. This book of Kung's drew not only on numerous scholarly precursors, but also on experiences with the problems of a global ethic especially at a UNESCO symposium in

Paris in 1989 on the topic 'No World Peace without Peace between the Religions' and the World Economic Forum in Davos in 1990, where the need for a global ethic was discussed in the context of the world religions and the world economy.[8]

The idea of a global ethic took on a surprisingly concrete and influential dimension at the **Parliament of the World's Religions** in Chicago in 1993. For the first time in the history of the religions the Council of the Parliament of the World's Religions had ventured on the development of a declaration on a global ethic. Hans Küng had undertaken this difficult task and with an international network of advisers in a complex consultative process had produced a definitive formulation.[9] As was only to be expected, this Declaration also prompted vigorous discussions during the Parliament, which was held from 28 August to 4 September. However, the welcome result was that in a time when so many religions are entangled in political conflicts and indeed in bloody wars, representatives of a variety of religions, great and small, have identified with this Declaration by signing it, as representatives of the 6,500 members of the Parliament from every possible religion, representing countless believers on this earth.

This Declaration Toward a Global Ethic gives expression to the common conviction that all men and women have a **responsibility for a better world order** and that commitment to human rights, to freedom, justice, peace and the preservation of the earth is urgently required.

The very different religious and cultural traditions must not be an obstacle to shared active commitment, against all forms of inhumanity and for greater humanity. The principles expressed in this Declaration can be accepted by all men and women with ethical convictions, whether these convictions have a religious basis or not.

The 1948 United Nations **Universal Declaration of**

88

Human Rights is explicitly recalled in the Declaration Toward a Global Ethic. What this declaration solemnly proclaimed on the level of **rights,** is to be endorsed and deepened from the perspective of **ethics:** the full realization of the sovereignty of human individuals and their inalienable freedom, the equality of all men and women in principle and their necessary solidarity and mutual interdependence.

However, the Declaration Toward a Global Ethic was not meant to be an end-point, a final agreement, but rather a prelude, a beginning and starting point for further dialogue between the religions and nations and within societies. That was clear from the start, and was once again specifically expressed at the end of the Parliament by the fact that this Declaration was termed an 'Initial Declaration Toward a Global Ethic'. This expressed the hope that the document could spark off a process which would change human behaviour in the religions and beyond in the direction of understanding, respect and collaboration.

III. In search of global ethical standards

The InterAction Council on the one hand and the sponsors of the Global Ethic Declaration on the other could certainly also have continued their concerns independently of one another. But a fruitful relationship developed, which had its starting point in the contact of two contemporaries who were already personally acquainted. Whereas the former Chancellor Helmut Schmidt was in search of 'universal human values' on behalf of the InterAction Council, through his study of the world religions Hans Küng, the professor of ecumenical theology, could already point to the results of research into a universal and generally binding ethic for humankind and the world.

Helmut Schmidt did not first engage intensively with the religions as Chairman of the InterAction Council. Above all personal encounters while he was Chancellor prompted him also to reflect on inter-religious questions. In his memoirs Schmidt keeps referring to a meeting with the Egyptian President Anwar el Sadat (1918-1981) which left a deep mark on him, and the 'exchange of ideas during a nocturnal journey up the Nile'. At the centre of Sadat's remarks was the so-called Abrahamic ecumene, i.e. the common origin of Judaism, Christianity and Islam in the God of Abraham, the 'Father of faith'.[10] For Sadat this common Abrahamic origin was as it were a vision of peace: 'Now we must at last reach back to what our faiths have in common in the one God ... Then peace between all three religions will be made possible.'[11]

'Sadat hoped for a great peaceful encounter between Judaism, Christianity and Islam ... Sadat's concern for peace derived from an understanding of and respect for the religions of others.'[12] Doubtless these encounters and reflections by Chancellor Helmut Schmidt also prompted him to occupy himself with inter-religious questions and questions of a global ethic within the framework of the InterAction Council, and to make efforts directed towards dialogue and peace between the religions.

In November 1995, Helmut Schmidt and **Hans Küng** made contact on the matter. After a lengthy telephone call, Schmidt wrote a long letter to Küng in which he reported on the work of the InterAction Council and mentioned two meetings of experts planned for Spring 1996. At the centre of one of these meetings was to be the question of 'human values' right across all the larger religious communities and philosophical traditions. In his letter Schmidt sought Küng's collaboration. He asked him for suggestions for the title of the meeting of experts and for the names of prominent representatives of Christianity, Judaism, Islam, Hinduism, Buddhism and Confucianism. At the end of his letter Helmut Schmidt emphasized that the plan of the InterAction Council came within the scope of Küng's work and aims, 'to emphasize a shared global ethic in the awareness that cultures are different'.

In his reply Küng accepted the invitation to collaborate. He suggested prominent representatives of various religions and in addition proposed 'In Search of a Global Ethic' as a title for the forthcoming meeting of experts. Two further questions could be introduced as supplementary sub-themes: 'What are moral standards for all humanity?' and 'What are trust- and peace-building measures between the world's religions?'

IV. Motive forces in Vienna (1996) and Vancouver (1996)

'In Search of Global Ethical Standards' was thus the title of the meeting of experts in **Vienna** from 22 to 24 March 1996 which took place under the chairmanship of Helmut Schmidt. As well as Schmidt, Andries van Agt (Netherlands), Pierre Trudeau (Canada) and Miguel de la Madrid (Mexico) took part as members of the InterAction Council. Hans Küng, Thomas Axworthy (Canada) and Kim Kyong-dong (South Korea) played a leading role at the Vienna conference as 'academic advisers'. Further scholars and spiritual dignitaries from all over the world represented Judaism, Christianity, Islam, Buddhism and Confucianism.[13]

The prime task of the 'High-level Expert Group' was to work out a discussion paper on the question of global ethical standards for the 1996 annual meeting of the InterAction Council in Vancouver. The topic of globalization was the basis for a diagnosis of the present. The religions as basic sources of ethical wisdom and directives towards activating collaboration in the solution of global problems were seen as a future hope for humankind. A series of precise questions led to the agenda of the Vienna Conference:

- First: a stocktaking of the international situation and the problems which call for special attention.
- Second: the identification of ethical standards which could be valid for the whole of humankind.
- Third: a description of the role which the religions could play in the search for global standards.
- Fourth: respect and recognition of the religious and cultural differences in the search for ethical standards and for means of promoting these.
- Fifth: a search for measures to build confidence and promote peace with a view to facilitating the dissemination and communication of global ethical standards.[14]

The **report**[15] which the body prepared as a basis for the Vancouver meeting of the InterAction Council was drafted by the academic advisers and was divided into four sections. After a general introduction which describes the upheavals in human civilization on the threshold of the twenty-first century and the confrontation with increasingly globalized problems, the section on **concrete measures**[16] (Kim Kyong-dong) emphasizes that the states – as agents of change – are to be regarded as the main audience and the main promoters of ethical standards; in addition attention also needs to be paid to the mass media and the transnational organizations, as these are increasingly gaining influence on global development. Thus in particular the religions of this world should be capable of working closely together in order to convince states and various important institutions of the need to implement and promote a global ethic. In view of the impending fiftieth anniversary of the 1948 UN Declaration of Human Rights, a Declaration of Human Responsibilities should be the topic of a conference.

In the chapter on the 'The Need for Global Ethical Standards' (Thomas Axworthy)[17] it is recalled that human social life depends on rules and guidelines. It is ethical standards which first make a harmonious collective life possible. Here the religions are particularly significant, and special attention needs to be paid to them: their fund of wisdom for humankind is needed more today than ever before. Ethics precedes politics and law, and therefore ethics must inform and inspire political leadership.

The spiritual resources and common ethical values of the religions are set out at length in the section on the '**Core of a Global Ethic**' (Hans Küng).[18] Here explicit reference is made to the 1993 **Chicago Declaration Toward a Global Ethic**. Thus the two basic principles which are fundamental to any individual, social and political ethic are commended: the basic requirement: 'Every human being must be treated humanely', and the Golden Rule: 'What you (do not) wish to be done to yourself, do (not do) to others.' In addition the 'four irrevocable directives' of the Chicago Declaration also found their way into the report:

- Commitment to a culture of non-violence and respect for life;
- Commitment to a culture of solidarity and a just economic order;
- Commitment to a culture of tolerance and a life of truthfulness;
- Commitment to a culture of equal rights and partnership between men and women.

The basic conviction of the report is expressed in one of its key statements: 'If we are to be able to solve the global problems, we must begin with a common ethical basis.'[19] Flora Lewis, the *International Herald Tribune* columnist, summed up the meeting of experts in Vienna by unmistakably bringing out its intention: 'Globalization brings a need for global ethics.' And finally she gave humankind something to reflect on in view of the complex global problems on the one hand

93

and the explosive increase of knowledge and capabilities on the other: 'We have learned how many things we can do. But we must attempt to learn again why.'[20]

The annual meeting of the InterAction Council then took place in Vancouver from 19 to 22 May 1996. It adopted the proposals from Vienna in its final communiqué[21] by summing up the Vienna report in a few paragraphs under the headings of globalization, the Chicago Declaration of the World Religions, making global ethical standards a major topic of public concern, and the fundamental significance of education in the context of global ethical values. Finally, it confirmed its basic conviction that 'ethics must precede politics and even law because political action is concerned with values and choices. Composed of former leaders well versed in the reality of power, the InterAction Council calls on the world's institutions to re-dedicate themselves to the primacy of normative ethical standards.'[22]

V. A global ethic on the world agenda

The efforts of the InterAction Council must not be seen in isolation. The requirement of a global ethic has been raised over recent years by various international conferences and commissions. The following statements are important.

1. The **UN Commission on Global Governance** produced a report on *Our Global Neighbourhood* (1995). Chapter II.3 calls for a global civil ethic: 'We therefore urge the international community to unite in support of a global ethic of common rights and shared responsibilities. In our view, such an ethic – reinforcing the fundamental rights that are already part of the fabric of international norms – would provide the moral foundation for constructing a more effective system of global governance.'[23]

94

2. The **World Commission on Culture and Development** published a report on *Our Creative Diversity* (1995). Chapter I describes a new global ethic:

'Co-operation between different peoples with different interests and from different cultures will be facilitated and conflicts kept within acceptable and even constructive limits, if participants can see themselves as being bound and motivated by shared commitments. It is, therefore, imperative to look for a core of shared ethical values and principles ... The idea is that the values and principles of a global ethic should be the shared points of reference, providing the minimal moral guidance the world must heed in its manifold efforts to tackle the global issues outlined above.'[24]

3. The **Third Millennium Project in Valencia** (in collaboration with UNESCO) presented a concluding report **Proposals for Future Orientation and Activities** (1997). Its conclusion, no. 15, says: 'To be sure, a globalized setting – not to speak of a new global order – demands the tacit or explicit acceptance of a set of global ethical principles. These principles should represent a minimum of global values for societies and nations to live together in harmony. We must secure conditions under which tolerance develops and various communities can co-exist. There can be no survival of humanity without a coalition of believers and non-believers in an atmosphere of mutual respect. Such principles could be complemented by a Charter of Citizens and the Rights and Duties of Nations.'[25]

4. The **World Economic Forum 1997 (Davos, Switzerland)** has similarly been active in these problems. In its press release of 4 February it states:

'The World Economic Forum aims to draft and achieve international consensus on a Declaration of Human Responsibilities. 'The notion of fundamental human rights has been with us for some time, but there is no similarly broad understanding of fundamental human obligations or responsibilities," said Forum Founder and President Klaus Schwab. "However, as globalization advances, a constructive international dialogue on common values and human obligations is a natural next step." A group of internationally prominent scholars of ethics and law convening at the annual meeting of the Forum said that a combination of continued violation of human rights around the world and the forces of globalization called for a new shared definition of ethical values and responsible human conduct.'[26]

5. The **1997 UNESCO Universal Ethics Project** held in **Paris** states in its final recommendations:
'Moral values and ethical principles that would form the core of a universal ethic are to be ascertained reflectively and empirically, that is, by identifying with and reflecting on those values and principles that are widely recognized and/or rationally necessary. The Project should accept as its starting point the work on universal rights, values and norms that has already been done.'[27]

6. The **Sixth Indira Gandhi Conference in Delhi (1997)** on **'Interdependencies and Identities in a Post-Colonial World'** formulates its conclusion under no.17:
'In a globalizing world undergoing a profound paradigm shift in beliefs, attitudes and behaviour of communities and individuals, the time may have come to work towards common, universal ethical principles where all religions and cultures agree. This may well serve as a basis for the formulation of a more far-reaching set of human duties, obligations and standards complementing and corresponding to the Universal Declaration of Human Rights. The observation of the 50th anniversary of the Universal Declaration would be an appropriate moment for such an initiative.'[28]

VI. A first draft: Vienna 1997

Hans Küng himself went more deeply into the problems in his 1997 book *A Global Ethic for Global Politics and Economics*. Here already there is reflection on the connection between human rights and human responsibilities.[29] Thus prepared, Küng could produce a **first draft** for the InterAction Council which in form and inspiration kept as closely as possible to the UN Declaration of Human Rights, but which in content and formulations was orientated above all on the 1993 Declaration of the Parliament of the World's Religions. Küng first of all sent the results of his efforts to the then President of the Council, Helmut Schmidt. After examining it, Schmidt felt that it could be presented to the group of experts in Vienna for discussion.

Of course those taking part in the **second Vienna meeting of experts between 20 and 22 April 1997** were surprised already to be confronted already with a detailed draft. So after the extended introduction by Küng there was an intensive and argumentative discussion about the content and form of the individual articles. For a while it seemed as if an alternative draft should be produced. But what initially seemed to be simple subsequently proved to be extremely difficult. The three academic advisers (Axworthy, Kim and Küng) finally agreed that the draft proposed by Küng was after all the best basis for further work, and this then also found general assent in the body of experts. Already in Vienna Axworthy and Küng incorporated various **desired changes** into the text and produced an improved version. Furthermore it was resolved to adopt the fundamental contribution on rights and responsibilities which had been prepared by the former President of Costa Rica, Oscar Arias Sánchez, Nobel Peace Prizewinner in 1987, in an abbreviated form as an **introduction to the document**.

The draft text which had already been worked over in

Vienna was then sent to the experts, who now had an opportunity to comment on its form and content: Küng also consulted further important advisors, some of whom had taken part in the first session of the UNESCO Universal Ethics Project in Paris in 1997.[30] He adapted the numerous **proposals for corrections** as far as possible and worked them into the text. Finally a document had come into being which could now be presented to the InterAction Council as a whole. This took place at the full meeting of the InterAction Council in Noordwijk, Netherlands, from 1 to 4 June 1997.

VII. Last polish and conclusion, Noordwijk 1997

In Noordwijk the InterAction Council had more to do than just pass judgment on the Universal Declaration of Human Responsibilities. The afternoon of 3 June 1997 had been set aside for this point on the agenda. There was a keen desire for Axworthy and Küng to take part in the whole session. However, because conferences of the Global Ethic Foundation were being held in Germany at the same time, Küng could be present in Noordwijk only in the afternoon and evening of 3 June.

The **discussion in the InterAction Council** developed dramatically. Every member had now been made aware by the draft text of what an important initiative had been taken and how far-reaching the consequences of such an enterprise would be. No fundamental opposition was expressed, but a number of reservations were indicated which made it seem hardly likely that the document would be approved in this session.

Questions of principle were raised: was it necessary to insert negative formulations (e.g. in Article 12: 'No one, however high and mighty, should speak lies') alongside the positive statements ('Every human being has a responsibility to speak and act truthfully')? Küng was given an opportunity to answer the objections. He emphasized that, for example, there was good reason why the biblical Ten Commandments were also formulated negatively; this was the only way of achieving the necessary precision, and politicians in particular were criticized in public for lying all too often. The argument continued, and various **alternatives** were considered: should the draft text be approved only as a discussion paper or as an interim report? Or should the whole document be sent as a stimulus to the individual governments? Or should the draft be revised? Or even should a special meeting of a drafting committee be arranged after Helsinki?

Finally there was agreement in the InterAction Council on the proposal of Andries van Agt, the chairman of the conference, that all members should have one more opportunity to study the present draft text in detail and sent **suggestions for improvement** or alternative suggestions within two months, by the end of July.

Andreis van Agt, Helmut Schmidt and Kurt Fugler were to be responsible for the **final redaction**. The work of redaction was delegated to Thomas Axworthy and Hans Küng. The latter accepted constructively the numerous suggestions and helpful proposals above all from Malcolm Fraser, the new President of the InterAction Council, and from Jimmy Carter, Maria de Lourdes Pintasiglio and Miguel de la Madrid Hurtado. In particular the positive statements were now put before the negative ones and 'human being' was replaced by 'human person'. Thus in the end a document was produced which maintained the basic structure and basic approach and all the essential statements of the previous draft but which was improved in many ways, in both form and content. The intense and argumentative discussion had finally proved extremely fruitful for the document. The permanent secretariat of the InterAction Council in Tokyo under Keiko Atsumi was a great help in the overall co-ordination.

At the beginning of August 1997 the definitive document

was presented to all the members of the InterAction Council for signature and finally found general assent. It was **published** by the new chairman, Malcolm Fraser, dated 1 September 1997 and sent simultaneously to the Secretary General of the United Nations, Kofi Annan, and to national governments throughout the world. The first publication was in English, German and Japanese. The Universal Declaration of Human Responsibilities is now available in sixteen further languages – a fact which demonstrates the interest in the Declaration and its dissemination and at the same time represents something new in the history of the InterAction Council: it has become the 'focus of international attention'.[31]

Notes

1. Right at the beginning I would like to express my thanks to Hans Küng, who has allowed me to look at archive material and in particular at his personal correspondence and filled in gaps in my knowledge by verbal comments. He is thus the one who has made this sketch of the process of the composition of the Universal Declaration of Human Responsibilities possible at all.
2. Much of the information about the InterAction Council appears in the conference dossier of the Noordwijk Forum held from 1 to 4 June 1997. H. Schmidt gives a very personal brief portrait of Takeo Fukuda and descriptions of the beginnings of the InterAction Council in his memoirs: *Weggefahrten. Erinnerungen und Reflexionen*, Berlin 1996, 307–16.
3. The following members of the InterAction Council took part in the meeting 'Spiritual Leaders Meet Political Leaders' at La Civiltà Cattolica: Takeo Fukuda (Japan); Helmut Schmidt (Germany), Jenoe Fock (Hungary), Malcolm Fraser (Australia), Olusegun Obasanjo (Nigeria), Misael Pastrana Borrero (Colombia), Maria de Lourdes Pintasiglio (Portugal) and Bradford Morse. The spiritual leaders were: A.T. Ariyaratne (Buddhism, Sri Lanka), K.H. Hasan Basri (Islam, Indonesia), John B. Cobb (Methodist Church, USA), Franz Cardinal König (Roman Catholic Church, Austria), Li Shu-pao (Protestant Church, China), Karan Singh (Hinduism, India), Eli Toaff (Judaism, Italy). Lester Brown (President of the Worldwatch Institute) was present as a representative of the sciences.
4. Documentation of the InterAction Council: *Peace, Development,*

Environment, Population. Spiritual Leaders Meet Political Leaders,
Rome 1987, Preface, 2.

5. 'Statement on Global Issues', ibid., 8ff.
6. H. Küng, *Global Responsibility* (1990), London and New York 1991.
7. Cf. especially H. Küng, J. van Ess, H. von Stietencron and H. Bechert, *Christianity and the World Religions,* New York 1986 and London 1987; H. Küng and J. Ching, *Christianity and Chinese Religion,* London and New York 1989.
8. The UNESCO Conference which took place in Paris on 8-10 February 1989 is comprehensively documented in H. Küng and K.-J. Kuschel (eds.), *Weltfrieden durch Religionsfrieden. Antworten aus den Weltreligionen,* Munich 1993.
9. Cf. H. Küng and K.-J. Kuschel (eds.), *A Global Ethic. The Declaration of the Parliament of the World's Religions,* London and New York 1993.
10. Cf. H. Schmidt, *Weggefährten* (n.1), 341f.
11. Ibid., 342.
12. Ibid., 343.
13. The following representatives were present: A. A. Mughram Al-Ghamdi (Islam, Great Britain), Shanti Aram (Hinduism, India), Abduljavad Falaturi (Islam, Iran), C. Ananda Grero (Buddhism, Sri Lanka), Franz Cardinal König (Roman Catholic Church, Austria), Peter Landesmann (Judaism, Austria), Liu Xiao-Feng (Confucianism, China), L.M. Singhvi (Jainism/India), Marjorie Suchocki (Protestantism, USA), Shizue Yamaguchi (observer, Japan).
14. Cf. the conference document *Terms of Reference for the High-level Group on 'In Search of Global Ethical Standards',* Vienna 22–24 March 1996.
15. Report on the Conclusions and Recommendations by a High-level Expert Group on 'In Search of Global Ethical Standards', chaired by H. Schmidt, 22–24 Marz 1996, Vienna.
16. Cf. ibid., 1f.
17. Cf. ibid, 3f.
18. Cf. ibid., 4f.
19. Ibid,., 4.
20. F. Lewis, 'Globalization Brings a Need for Global Ethics', *International Herald Tribune,* 28 March 1996.
21. Cf. *Communiqué of the InterAction Council 14th Session, 19–22 May 1996, Vancouver, BC, Canada,* 3.
22. Ibid. 3.
23. The Commission on Global Governance, *Our Global Neighbourhood,* Oxford 1995, 56. This commission derives from an initiative by the former German Chancellor Willy Brandt and was founded in 1992 with the support of the Secretary General of the United Nations, Boutros Boutros-Ghali. The chairmen are: Ingvar Carlsson (Sweden), Shridath Ramphal (Guyana). Members: Ali Alatas (Indonesia). Abdlatif Al-Hamad (Kuwait), Oscar Arias (Costa Rica), Anna Balletbo i Puig (Spain), Kurt Biedenkopf (Germany), Allan Boesak (South Africa),

Manuel Camacho Solis (Mexico), Bernard Chidzero (Zimbabwe), Barber Conable (United States of America), Jaques Delors (France), Jiri Dienstbier (Czech Republic), Enrique Iglesias (Uruguay), Frank Judd (Great Britain), Lee Hong-koo (Republic of Korea), Wangari Maathai (Kenya), Sadako Ogata (Japan), Olara Otunnu (Uganda), I.G. Patel (India), Celina Vargas do Amaral Peixoto (Brazil), Jan Pronk (Netherlands), Qian Jiadong (China), Marie-Angélique Savané (Senegal), Adele Simmons (United States of America), Maurice Strong (Canada), Brian Urquhart (Great Britain), Yuli Vorontsov (Russia). General Secretary: Hans Dahlgren.

24. Report of the World Commission on Culture and Development, *Our Creative Diversity*, Paris 1995, 34f. President: Javier Pérez de Cuéllar (Peru). Honorary Members: Crown Prince El Hassan Bin Talal (Jordan), Aung San Suu Kyi (Burma), Claude Lévi-Strauss (France), Ilya Prigogine (Belgium), Derek Walcott (Santa Lucia), Elie Wiesel (United States of America). Members: Lourdes Arizpe (Mexico), Yoro Fall (Senegal), Kurt Furgier (Switzerland), Celso Furtado (Brazil), Niki Goulandris (Greece), Keith Griffin (Great Britain), Mahhub ul Haq (Pakistan), Elizabeth Jelin (Argentina), Angeline Kamba (Zimbabwe), Ole-Henrik Magga (Norway), Nikita Mikhalkov (Russia), Chie Nakane (Japan), Leila Takla (Egypt). Executive Secretary: Yudhishthir Raj Isar (India).

25. Final Report: *Proposals for the Future Orientation and Activities of the Third Millennium Project, Valencia, 23 to 25 January 1997* (in collaboration with UNESCO). A number of distinguished representatives of science, culture and politics came to Valencia for exchanges and discussion on a wide-ranging and varied spectrum of topics. They included: Karl-Otto Apel (Germany), Diego Cordovez (Ecuador), Jiri Dienstbier (Czech Republic), Hans Erni (Switzerland), Richard Falk (USA), Eiji Hattori (Japan), Hans Küng (Switzerland), Wolfgang Leonhard (Germany), Flora Lewis (USA), Dragoljub Najam (Yugoslavia), Hans d'Orville (Germany), Unsung Kenneth Park (Korea), K. Natwar Singh (India), Ola Ullsten (Sweden), Sir Peter Ustinov (Great Britain), Mario Vargas Llosa (Peru), George Vassiliou (Cyprus).

26. Press release from the World Economic Forum 1997 (Davos, Switzerland), 4 February. The following took part in the Working Group on 'Rights and Responsibilities': Ahmed Kamal Abulmagd (Egypt), Roger Cardinal Etchegaray (Vatican), Amitai Etzioni (USA), Kay R. Jamison (USA), Alois Jelonek (Germany), Hans Küng (Germany), Bernard Lewis (USA), Shimon Peres (Israel), Elie Wiesel (USA) und Patrick Glynn (USA).

27. Recommendations of the UNESCO Universal Ethics Project, which held its first meeting in Paris in March 1997. Taking part in the conference were: Karl-Otto Apel (Germany), Aziz Al-Azmeh (Syria), Sissela Bok (USA), Osvaldo Guariglia (Argentina), Paulin Hountondji (Benin), Ionanna Kuçuradi (Turkey), Hans Küng (Germany), Lin Shu-hsien (Hong Kong), Jacques Poulain (France), Leonard Swidler (USA),

Karan Singh (India), Michael Walzer (USA) and Kim Yersu (South Korea) in the chair.

28. *Draft Conclusions. Sixth Indira Gandhi Conference: Post Colonial World: Interdependence and Identities, New Delhi, India, 20–22 November 1997.*

29. H. Küng, *A Global Ethic for Global Politics and Economics*, London 1997 and New York 1998, 99–104.

30. In addition to suggestions from Sissela Bok (USA), Lin Shu-hsien (Hong Kong), Leonard Swidler (USA), Karan Singh (India), and Michael Walzer (USA), who took part in the UNESCO Universal Ethics Project in Paris, Hans Küng was also able to incorporate suggestions by Julia Ching (Canada) and Karl-Josef Kuschel (Germany) into the revised text.

31. Thus the General Secretary of the InterAction Council, Isamu Miyazaki, in his circular letter of 21 November 1997.

Don't Be Afraid of Ethics!

Why we need to talk of responsibilities as well as rights

HANS KÜNG

'Is he afraid of ethics?' Not very long ago my dear friend Alfred Grosser, the political theorist from Paris, whispered this question in my ear. The occasion was a televised dispute in Baden Baden, in which the presenter was once again gallantly dismissing the question of ethics with a reference to more immediate issues. This question came home to me again on reading the first contributions to the discussion on the proposal for a **Universal Declaration of Human Responsibilities.**[1] As one of the three 'academic advisers' to the Inter-Action Council, which is made up of former heads of states and governments, I was responsible not only for the first draft of this declaration but also for incorporating the numerous corrections suggested by the statesmen and the many experts from different continents, religions and disciplines. I therefore identify completely with the declaration. However, had I not been occupied for years with the problems, and had I not finally written *A Global Ethic for Global Politics and Global Economics*, published in 1997, which provides a broad treatment of all the problems which arise here, I would not have dared to formulate a first draft at all – in close conjunction with the 1948 Declaration of Human Rights and the 1993 Declaration Toward a Global Ethic endorsed by the Parliament of the World's Religions, which required a secular political continuation. I say this simply to those who presuppose great naivety behind such declarations. That is certainly not the case!

1. Globalization calls for a global ethic

1. The declaration by the InterAction Council (IAC) is not an isolated document. It meets the **urgent call by important international bodies** for global ethical standards at present made in chapters of the reports both of the UN Commission on Global Governance (1995) and the World Commission on Culture and Development (1995). The same topic has also already been discussed for a long time at the World Economic Forum (WEF) in Davos and similarly in the new UNESCO Universal Ethics Project. Increasing attention is also being paid to it in Asia.[2]

2. The contemporary background to the questions raised in these international and interreligious bodies is the fact that the **globalization** of the economy, technology and the media has also brought a globalization of their problems (from the financial and labour markets to ecology and organized crime). If there are to be global solutions to them, they therefore also call for a **globalization of ethics**: no uniform ethical system, but a necessary minimum of shared ethical values, basic attitudes and criteria to which all regions, nations and interest groups can commit themselves. In other words there is a need for a common basic human ethic. There can be no new world order without a world ethic.

3. All this is not based on an 'alarmist' analysis but on a **realistic analysis of society**. Critics have selected a few isolated quotations in particular from Helmut Schmidt's introductory article on the Declaration of Human Responsibilities in *Die Zeit*, printed here, and constructed a twofold charge from it:

(a) the analysis of society underlying the Declaration is purely negative, gloomy, and orientated on decline;

(b) such 'gloomy pictures of society' would be used in 'potentially successful' campaigns to 'supplement individual freedoms by reinforcing communal obligations', a suspicion which culminates in the charge that all this would be done 'to limit the consequences of these individual freedoms'. Over against this, emphatic reference is made to empirical investigations which are said to have discovered that there has been no 'repudiation of and decline in' morality. As if Helmut Schmidt had asserted any of this! As if he had engaged in sheer 'alarmism', demonized individualism, lamented a decline in values ...! Instead of this, Schmidt has indicated in a sober and realistic way some elements of danger in the process of globalization which have been seen and complained about for a long time all over the world. And Schmidt's plea for a Declaration of Human Responsibilities in particular presupposes that there are sufficient people also in the younger generation who at least in principle affirm 'responsibility', 'morality' and 'orientation on the common good'. However, hardly anyone can seriously dispute that after the increase in and reinforcement of the rights of the individual over the past three decades, we need a stocktaking of education, journalism and politics. For:

4. A sober diagnosis of the present notes that the radicalized individualization, accelerated secularization and ideological pluralization of present society is not just a negative development (thus the Vatican hierarchy), nor is it just a positive development (thus the belated representatives of the modern Enlightenment), but a highly ambivalent structural change. It brings opportunities and advantages, but also enormous risks and dangers, and in the midst of a revolutionary change raises new questions **about criteria for values and points of orientation**. This does not mean 'turning back the clock', but recognizing the 'signs of the times'. As Marion Countess Dönhoff has remarked: 'Of course pluralistic democracy is unthinkable without the autonomous individual. So

there can be no question of turning our backs on emancipation and secularization – moreover that would be impossible. What we have to do is to educate citizens to greater responsibility and again give them a sense of solidarity. In our present world with its manifold temptations and attractions, the desire for a basic moral orientation, for norms and a binding system of values, is very great. Unless we take account of that, this society will not hold together.'[3] Ralf Dahrendorf makes the following observation on the 'question of law and order', which for him is one of the 'great questions of our time', along with unemployment and the welfare state. 'Lawlessness is the scourge of modernity. The sense of belonging disappears, and with it is lost the support which a strong civil society gives to individuals and which they can take for granted. There is little to indicate why existing regulations and laws should be observed. Police control can replace social control only at the price of becoming authoritarian or, even worse, totalitarian. What holds modern society together?'[4]

5. The question of **what holds society together** has in fact become more acute in postmodernity, which is a new epoch-making paradigm and does not just amount to a 'second modernity'. For:

– On the one hand a classic statement which the constitutional lawyer E.-W. Böckenförde made at a very early stage is still true: 'The free secular state lives on the basis of presuppositions which it cannot guarantee without putting its freedom in question.'[5] Modern society therefore needs leading social and political ideas which emerged from common convictions, attitudes and traditions that would predate this freedom. These resources are not naturally there, but need to be looked after, aroused and handed down by education ('Responsibilities are not there "just like that"').

– But on the other hand, what the sociologist H. Dubiel, among others, has emphasized is also true. The modern liberal social order has for a long time relied on 'habits of the heart', on a thick cushion of pre-modern systems of meaning and obligation, though today – as is also confirmed by many teachers of religion and ethics – these are now 'worn out'.[6]

6. So what will hold post-modern society together? Certainly **not religious fundamentalism** of a biblicistic Protestant or a Roman Catholic kind. In the Declaration of Human Responsibilities there is deliberately not a single word about questions like birth control, abortion or euthanasia, on which there cannot be a consensus between and within the churches and religions. **Nor**, however, will society be held together by the **random pluralism** which wants to sell us indifferentism, consumerism and hedonism as a 'post-modern' vision of the future. **But** in the end the only thing that will hold society together is a new **basic social consensus** on shared values and criteria, which combines autonomous self-realization with responsibility in solidarity, rights with obligations. So we should not be afraid of an ethic which can be supported by quite different social groups. What we need is a fundamental **yes to morality** as a moral attitude, combined with a decisive **no to moralism**, which one-sidedly insists firmly on particular moral positions (e.g. on sexuality).

II. Human responsibilities reinforce human rights

1. Individual human rights activists who have evidently been surprised by the new problems and the topicality of human responsibilities initially reacted with perplexity to the proposal for a Declaration of Responsibilities. Here I am not speaking of those one-issue people who with Jeremiads and scenarios of destruction force all the problems of the world under a single perspective (say the intrinsically justified perspective of ecology, or any other perspective that they regard as the sum and solution of all the problems of the world), and who want to force their one-dimensional, often monocausal view, of the world (Carl Amery's 'biospheric perspective')

upon everyone, instead of taking seriously the many levels and the many dimensions of human life and social reality, as the Declaration on Human Responsiblities does. I am speaking, rather, of those who use sophisticated arguments, like the German General Secretary of Amnesty International, Volkmar Deile.[7] In principle he affirms 'a necessary minimum of shared ethical values, basic attitudes and criteria to which all religions, nations and interest groups can commit themselves', but he has suspicions about a separate Declaration of Human Responsibilities. These suspicions seeem to me to be worth considering, even if in the end I cannot share them. The main reason is that a Declaration of Human Responsibilities does not do the slightest damage to the Declaration of Human Rights. At any rate the UN Commissions and other international bodies cited here[8] are of the same opinion. Reflection on human responsibilities does not damage the realization of human rights. On the contrary, it furthers it. But let us look more closely.

2. A Declaration of Human Responsibilities **supports and reinforces the Declaration of Human Rights from an ethical perspective**, as is already stated programmatically in the preamble: 'We thus ... renew and reinforce commitments already proclaimed in the Universal Declaration of Human Rights: namely, the full acceptance of the dignity of all people; their inalienable freedom and equality, and their solidarity with one another.' If human rights are not realized in many places where they could be implemented, this is for the most part for want of a lack of political and ethical will. There is no disputing the fact that 'the rule of law and the promotion of human rights depend on the readiness of men and women to act justly'. Nor will any of those who fight for human rights dispute this.

3. Of course it would be wrong to think that the legal validity of human rights depends on the actual realization of responsibilities. 'Human rights – a reward for good human

behaviour': who would assert such nonsense? This would in fact mean that only those who had shown themselves worthy of rights by doing their duty towards society would have any. That would clearly offend against the unconditional **dignity of the human person,** which is itself a presupposition of both rights and responsibilities. No one has claimed that certain human responsibilities must be fulfilled **first,** by individuals or a community, before one can claim human rights. These are given with the human person, but this person is **always at the same time one who has rights and responsibilities:** 'All human rights are by definition directly bound up with the responsibility to observe them' (V.Deile). Rights and responsibilities can certainly be distinguished neatly, but they cannot be separated from one another. Their relationship needs to be described in a differentiated way. They are not quantities which are to be added or subtracted externally, but **two related dimensions** of being human in the individual and the social sphere.

4. **No rights without responsibilities:** as such, this concern is by no means new, but goes back to the 'founding period' of human rights. The demand was already made in the debate over human rights in the French Revolutionary Parliament of 1789 that if one proclaims a Declaration of Human **Rights** one must combine it with a Declaration of Human **Responsibilities.** Otherwise, in the end everyone would have only rights, which they would play off against one another, and no one would any longer know the responsibilities without which these rights cannot function. And what about us, 200 years after the great Revolution? We in fact live largely in a society in which individual groups all too often insist on **rights against others** without recognizing any **responsibilities** that they themselves have. This is certainly not because of codified human rights as such, but because of certain false developments closely connected with them. In the consciousness of many people these have led to a preponderance of

rights over responsibilities. Instead of the culture of human rights which is striven for, there is often an unculture of exaggerated claims to rights which ignores the intentions of human rights. The 'equilibrium of freedom, equality and participation' is not simply 'present', but time and again has to be realized afresh. After all, we indisputably live in a 'society of claims', which often presents itself as a 'society of legal claims', indeed as a 'society of legal disputes'. This makes the state a 'judiciary state' (a term applied to the Federal Republic of Germany by the legal historian S. Simon).[9] Does this not suggest the need for a new concentration on responsibilities, particularly in our over-developed constitutional states with all their justified insistence on rights?

5. What Deile calls 'the reality of severe violations of human rights which spans the world' should make it clear, particularly to professional champions of human rights who want to defend human rights 'unconditionally', how much a declaration and explanation of human rights comes up against a void where people, particularly those in power, ignore ('What concern is that of mine?), neglect ('I have to represent only the interests of my firm'), fail to perceive ('That's what churches and charities are for'), or simply pretend falsely to be fulfilling ('We, the government, the board of directors, are doing all that we can), their human responsibilities. The 'weakness of human rights' is not in fact grounded in the concept itself 'but in the lack of any political (and – I would add – moral) will on the part of those responsible for implementing them' (V. Deile). To put it plainly: **an ethical impulse and the motivation of norms is needed for an effective realization of human rights**. Many human rights champions active on the fronts of this world who confess their 'Yes to a Global Ethic'[10] have already explicitly endorsed that. Therefore those who want to work effectively for human rights should welcome a new moral impulse and

framework of ethical orientation and not reject it, to their own disadvantage.

6. The **framework of ethical orientation** in the Declaration of Human Responsibilities in some respects extends beyond human rights, which now 'clearly say what is commanded and forbidden only for quite specific spheres' (V. Deile). Nor does the Declaration of Human Rights expressly raise such a comprehensive moral claim. A Declaration of Human Responsibilities must extend much further and begin at a much deeper level. And indeed the two basic principles of the Declaration of Human Responsibilities already offer an ethical orientation of everyday life which is as comprehensive as it is fundamental: the basic demand, 'Every human being must be treated humanely', and the Golden Rule, 'What you do not wish to be done to yourself, do not do to others'. Not to mention the concrete requirements of the Declaration of Responsibilities for truthfulness, non-violence, fairness, solidarity, partnership, etc. Where the Declaration of Human Rights has to leave open what is morally permissible and what is not, the Declaration of Human Responsibilities states this – not as a law but as a moral imperative. Therefore the Declaration of Human Responsibilities 'opens up the possibility of agreement – democratic agreement – about what is right and wrong, what is permissible and what is forbidden, indeed even what is right and what is wrong. The manifesto returns the responsibility of being interested in these important questions to the individual. Thus it is not paternalistic but political. What else could it be?'[11]

7. If the Declaration of Human Responsibilities is mostly formulated 'anonymously', since it is focussed less on the individual (to be protected) than on the state (the power of which has to be limited), while the Declaration of Human Responsibilities is also addressed to state and institutions, it is primarily and very **directly addressed to responsible persons**. Time and again it says 'all people' or 'every person';

indeed specific professional groups which have a particular responsibility in our society (politicians, officials, business leaders, writers, artists, doctors, lawyers, journalists, religious leaders) are explicitly addressed, but no one is singled out. It is beyond dispute that such a Declaration of Responsibilities represents a challenge in the age of random pluralism, at least for the 'winners' in the process of individualization at the expense of others, and for all those who recognize only 'provided it's fun' or 'it contributes to my personal development' as the sole moral norm. But the declaration is not concerned with a new 'community ideology', which is the criticism made of the communitarians around Amitai Etzioni. At least these people do not want to set up a 'tyranny of the common mind' and to relieve people even of individual responsibility. That is what is done, rather, by their superficially moral opposite numbers, who, fatally mistaking the crisis of the present, think that they have to propagate a 'confession of the selfish society' or the 'virtue of having no orientation or ties' as a way into the future.

8. Thus like the Declaration of Human Rights, the Declaration of Human Responsibilities is primarily a **moral appeal**. As such it does not have the direct binding character of international law, but it proclaims to the world public some basic norms for collective and individual behaviour which apply to everyone. This appeal is, of course, also meant to have an effect on legal and political practice. However, it does not aim at any legalistic morality. The Declaration of Responsibilities is not a 'blueprint for a legally binding canon of responsibilities with a world-wide application', as has been insinuated. No such spectres should be conjured up at a time when even the pope and the curial apparatus can no longer implement their legalistic authoritarian moral views in their very own sphere (far less in the outside world). A key feature of the Declaration of Human Responsibilities is that it specifically **does not aim at legal codification**, which in any

case is impossible in the case of moral attitudes like truthfulness or fairness. It aims at **voluntarily taking responsibility**. Such a declaration can of course lead to legal regulations in individual cases, or if it is applied to institutions. However, a Declaration of Human Responsibilities should be said to be **morally** rather than **legally** binding.

III. 'Responsibilities' can be misused – but so too can 'rights'

1. Particularly those who reject any revision of the Declaration of Human Rights (and this is certainly also rejected by the IAC) should argue for a Declaration of Human Responsibilities. To discredit the plea of many **Asians** for a recognition of responsibilities – traditional in Confucianism, Hinduism, Buddhism and Islam – a priori as authoritarian and paternalistic is to be blind to reality and arrogant in a Eurocentric way. It is obvious that here the attack on the idea of responsibilities is often governed by political interests. But that does not deprive the demand for **responsibilities** generally of its credibility, any more than the call for **freedom** is discredited because it is misused by robber baron capitalists or sensational journalists. To think that authoritarian systems would wait specifically for a Declaration of Responsibilities and in the future too would be dependent on a Declaration of Responsibilities to uphold their authoritarian system is ridiculous. Rather, in the future it will be possible to address authoritarian systems more critically than before over their responsibility to show truthfulness and tolerance – which is not contained in any human rights. And this can have an effect. Authoritarian systems like those of Poland, the German Democratic Republic, Czechoslovakia, the Soviet Union, the Philippines or South Africa were overthrown without bloodshed, not least by moral arguments and demonstrations, with demands for

'truth', 'freedom', 'justice', 'solidarity', humanity', slogans which often went beyond human rights. So human rights and human responsibilities should be seen together. A Declaration of Human Responsibilities can serve many people as a **reference document** in the same way as the Declaration of Human Rights – and this can be significant not least for education and schools.

2. Germans in particular do have an additional problem here. Unfortunately they do not have the good fortune of the Anglo-Americans, who have three related terms with different emphases, **'duties', 'obligations' and 'responsibilities'**, where they have to make do with **one, 'Pflicht'**. It was exciting to see how the professionals both in Paris (UNESCO) and Vienna (InterAction Council) and in Davos (World Economic Forum) each time quickly agreed on the term 'responsibilities' to translate *Pflicht*. Why? Because this term more than the other words emphasizes inner responsibility rather than the external law, and inner responsibility must be the ultimate aim of a Declaration of Responsibilities, which can in no way enforce an ethic. If *Verantwortlichkeit* were accepted terminology, that would have been preferable, but it seemed possible to use this only on isolated occasions.

3. Europeans, and especially Germans, need to be reminded that this term *Pflicht* in the sense of 'duty' has been **shamefully misused** in their more recent history. 'Duty' (towards superiors, the Führer, the Volk, the party, even the pope) has been hammered home by totalitarian, authoritarian and hierarchical ideologies of all kinds. So one can understand the anxious projections ('authoritarian state', 'paternalism' ...), which have led to the word being made morally and ultimately even linguistically taboo. But should abuses prevent us from taking up positively a concept which has had a long history since Cicero and Ambrose, which was made a **key concept of modern times,** and which even today seems irreplaceable? So we should not be afraid of ethics:

responsibility exerts a moral pressure but it does not compel. It follows primarily not from purely technical or economic reason but from **ethical reason**, which **encourages** and urges **human beings,** whose nature it is to be able to decide freedom, **to act morally.** And here it should be remembered that:

4. Not only responsibilities but **also rights can be misused,** particularly when, **first,** they are constantly used exclusively for one's own advantage and, **secondly,** when they are constantly exploited to the maximum, to the limit of their own extreme possibilities. Those who neglect their responsibilities finally also undermine rights. Even the state would be endangered if its citizens made no meaningful use of rights and employed them purely to their own advantage. Indeed, not even Amnesty International could survive if it was governed and supported by such egotistic 'being in the right' instead of by ethically motivated activists. So we should be aware of false alternatives:

5. Liberating rights (in the West) versus enslaving responsibilities (in the East): this is a construction against which resolute opposition must be declared. The Declaration of Responsibilities which reinforces the Declaration of Rights could perceive a function of supplementing and mediating here – without threatening the universal validity, the indivisibility and the cohesion of human rights. It could be a help towards avoiding a 'clash of civilizations' which only the innocent can suppose to be 'long refuted'.

6. I share the love of **freedom,** and Isaiah Berlin was certainly right in saying that freedom is essentially about the absence of compulsion with the 'negative' aim of avoiding interference: i.e. freedom from. But as a former Isaiah Berlin lecturer in Cambridge, perhaps I may modestly remark that a pure 'freedom **from**' can be destructive and sometimes dangerous without a 'freedom **for**'; here the British sociologist Anthony Giddens confirms a piece of old theological wisdom. This should certainly not be a call for the exercise of

freedom 'as service to the community', which can easily lead to servitude, but is rather that freedom in responsibility without which **liberty becomes libertinism**, which in the end leaves people who live only for their egos inwardly burnt out. However, such libertinism becomes a social problem the moment there is a dramatic increase in the number of people who selfishly cultivate their own interests and the private aesthetic development of their everyday lives, and are ready for commitment only in so far as this serves their needs and sense of pleasure. Even the political weeklies and journals are slowly beginning to note this: recently major critical articles have appeared on 'The Shameless Society' or 'The New Shamelessness'.

7. We need not worry: **morality and community** cannot be 'prescribed' as obligations. And the best guarantee of peace is in fact a functioning state which guarantees its citizens the security of the law. Here human rights are the 'guiding star' (not the 'explosive device') of such a society. But precisely because community and morality cannot be prescribed, the personal responsibility of its citizens is indispensable. As we saw, the democratic state is dependent on a consensus of values, norms and responsibilities, precisely because it cannot and should not either create this consensus or prescribe it.

8. Those concerned with human rights in particular must know that the **Declaration of Human Rights itself, in Article 29,** contains a definition of the 'duties of everyone towards the community'. From this it follows with compelling logic that a Declaration of Human Responsibilities cannot in any way stand in contradiction to the Declaration of Human Rights. And if concrete forms of political, social and cultural articles on human rights were possible and necessary through international agreements in the 1960s, why should a development of Article 29 by an extended formulation of these responsibilities in the 1990s be illegitimate? On the contrary, precisely in the light of this it becomes clear that human rights

and human responsibilities **do not mutually restrict** each other for society **but supplement each other in a fruitful way** – and all champions of human rights should recognize this as a reinforcement of their position. It is not by chance that this Article 29 speaks of the 'just requirements of morality, public order and general welfare in a democratic society'. But the asymmetrical structure in the determination of the relationship of rights and responsibilities must be noted.

IV. Not all responsibilities follow from rights

1. The decisive question, whether expressed or not, is whether alongside a claim to rights there is also a need for reflection on responsibilities. The answer to that is: all rights imply responsibilities, but **not all responsibilities follow from rights**. Here are three examples:

(a) The **freedom of the press** or of a journalist is guaranteed and protected by the modern constitutional state: the journalist, the newspaper, has the **right** to report freely. The state must protect this right actively, and if need be enforce it. Therefore the state and the citizen have the **responsibility** of respecting the right of this newspaper or this journalist to free reporting. However, this right does not yet in any way touch on the **responsibility of the journalist or the media themselves** (which has been widely discussed since the death of Princess Diana) to inform the public truthfully and avoid sensational reporting which demeans the dignity of the human person (cf. Article 14 of the Declaration of Responsibilities). But that the freedom of opinion which critics claim entails a responsibility 'not to insult others' is a claim to which no lawyer would subscribe.[12]

(b) The **right** of each individual **to property** is also guaranteed by the modern constitutional state. It entails the legal **responsibility** of others (the state or the individual citizen) to

118

respect this property and not to misappropriate it. However, this right does not in any way affect the **responsibility of property-owners themselves** not to use the property in an anti-social way but to use it socially (this is laid down as a duty in the German Basic Law), to bridle the manifestly unquenchable human greed for money, power, prestige and consumption, and to use economic power in the service of social justice and social order (cf. Article 11).

(c) The **freedom of conscience** of individuals to decide in accordance with their own consciences contains the legal **responsibility** of themselves and others (individuals and the state) to respect any free decision of the conscience: the individual conscience is guaranteed protection by the constitution in democracies. However, this right by no means entails the **ethical responsibility of individuals** to follow their own conscience in every case, even, indeed precisely when this is unacceptable or abhorrent to them.

2. It follows from this that rights also entail certain responsibilities, and these are **legal responsibilities**. But by no means all responsibilities follow from rights. There are also independent **ethical responsibilities** which are directly grounded in the dignity of the human person. At a very early stage in the theoretical debate on this, **two types of responsibility** were distinguished: obligations in the narrower sense, 'complete', **legal obligations**; and responsibilities in the wider sense, 'incomplete', **ethical responsibilities** like those prompted by conscience, love and humanity. These are based on the insight of the individual and cannot be compelled by the state through law.

3. Thus ethics is not exhausted in law. The **levels of law and ethics** belong together, but **a fundamental distinction is to be made between them**, and this is particularly significant for human rights.

– Human beings have fundamental rights which are formulated in the Declarations of Human Rights. To these correspond the legal responsibilities of both the state and individual citizens to respect and protect these rights. Here we are at the **level of law**, regulations, the judiciary, the police. External behaviour in conformity to the law can be examined; in principle the law can be appealed to and if need be enforced ('in the name of the law').

– But at the same time human beings have original responsibilities which are already given with their personhood and are not grounded in any rights: these are ethical responsibilities which cannot be fixed by law. Here we are at the **level of ethics**, customs, the conscience, the 'heart' ... The inward, morally good disposition, or even truthfulness, cannot be tested directly; therefore it cannot be brought under the law, let alone be compelled ('thoughts are free'). The 'sanctions' of the conscience are not of a legal kind but often of a moral kind – and can even be felt in dreams and sleeplessness. The fact that immorality rarely pays in the long run, even in politics and business, and often leads to conflicts with the criminal law, does not follow directly from the ethical imperative.

4. **Where a gap yawns between law and ethics**, the law does not function either. Whether human rights will be realized in concrete terms depends not only generally on the ethical will of those responsible, but often on the moral energy of an individual or a few people. Even the realization of the fundamental principle of international law, *pacta sunt servanda*, 'treaties are to be kept', depends quite decisively on the ethical will of the partner to the treaty, as the example of former Yugoslavia has again demonstrated. And must not truthfulness, which cannot be tested by the law, be presupposed in the conclusion of any treaty, even if it cannot be compelled legally? 'Morality is good, rights are better' (as Norbert Greinacher remarked) is a simple statement. For what use are any rights or laws if there are no morals, no moral disposition, no obligation of conscience behind them?

In other words, the **law needs a moral foundation!** So the Declaration of Responsibilities says that a better world order cannot be created with laws, conventions and ordinances alone. Indeed, without an ethic, in the end the law will not stand. So it is meaningful and requisite to set a Declaration of Human Responsibilities alongside the Declaration of Human Rights. As I have remarked, the two do not restrict each other but support each other.

5. One last thing: the nineteen articles of the Declaration of Responsibilities are anything but a random cocktail. As any expert will easily recognize, they are a **reshaping of the four elementary imperatives of humanity** (not to kill, steal, lie, commit sexual immorality) translated for our time. Despite all the differences between the faiths, these can already be found in Patanjali, the founder of Yoga, the Bhagavadgita and the Buddhist canon, and of course also in the Hebrew Bible, the New Testament, the Qur'an, and indeed in all the great religious and ethical traditions of humankind. No 'cultural relativism' is being encouraged here; rather, this is overcome by the integration of culture-specific values into an ethical framework with a universal orientation. As we saw, like human rights, these fundamental human responsibilities have their point of reference, their centre and the nucleus in the acknowledgment of **human dignity**, which stands at the centre of the very first sentence of the Declaration of Human Responsibilities, as it does in the Declaration of Human Rights. From it follows the fundamental ethical imperative to treat every human being humanely, made concrete by the Golden Rule, which also does not express a right but a responsibility. Thus the Declaration of Responsibilities is an appeal to the institutions, but also to the moral consciousness of individuals, explicitly to note the ethical dimension in all action.

6. My **final wish** for the wider debate is for there to be no false fronts, no artificial oppositions between rights and

responsibilities, between an ethic of freedom and an ethic of responsibility, but rather a grasping of the opportunities which there could be in such a perhaps epoch-making declaration, were it promulgated. After all, it is not every day that statesmen from all the continents agree on such a text and propagate such a cause. And above all let us not be afraid of ethics: rightly understood, ethics does not enslave but frees. It helps us to be truly human and to remain so.

Notes

1. Cf. the series on rights and responsibilies in *Die Zeit*, nos 41–48, 1997. Contributors included Helmut Schmidt, Constanze Stelzenmüller, Thomas Kleine-Brockhoff, Susanne Gaschke, Volkmar Deile, Hans Küng, Norbert Greinacher, Carl Amery and Marion Countess Donhoff. Where names appear in this article without further details they usually refer to this series.
2. Cf. the contribution by J. Frühbauer in this volume.
3. Marion Countess Dönhoff, 'Verantwörtung für das Ganze', in E. Teufel (ed.), *Was hält die moderne Gesellschaft zusammen?*, Frankfurt 1996, 44. Or Thomas Assheuer, addressing the naively optimistic propagandists of a 'second modernity' (Ulrich Beck): 'To speak of a social and moral crisis is no longer the privilege of conservatives' (T. Assheuer, 'Im Prinzip ohne Hoffnung. Die "zweite Moderne" als Formel: Wie Soziologen alte Fragen neue drapieren', *Die Zeit*, 18 July 1997).
4. R. Dahrendorf, 'Liberale ohne Heimat', *Die Zeit*, 8 January 1998.
5. Thus the federal judge E.-W. Böckenförde, 'Fundamente der Freiheit', in Teufel (ed.), *Was hält die moderne Gesellschaft zusammen?* (n.3), 89. Böckenförde formulated the thesis quoted above thirty years ago, and in the meantime it may be taken to have been fully accepted.
6. H. Dubiel, 'Von welchen Ressourcen leben wir? Erfolge und Grenzen der Aufklärung', ibid., 81.
7. Cf. V. Deile, 'Rechte bedingungslos verteidigen', *Die Zeit*, 21 November 1997.
8. There are more details in J. Fruhbauer's article, above 84–103.
9. Cf. the radio broadcast by the Director of the Max Planck Institute for European Legal History in Frankfurt am Main, D. Simon, 'Der Richter als Ersatzkaiser' (manuscript).
10. Cf. H. Küng (ed.) *Yes to a Global Ethic*, London and New York 1996.
11. S. Gaschke, 'Die Ego-Polizei', *Die Zeit*, 24 October 1997.
12. For this complex of problems see the correspondence between the World Press Freedom Committee and the InterAction Council, below, 134–40.

International Reactions

I. The United Nations Organization

Letter of Response by the Secretary General, Kofi Annan

The General Secretary   16 September 1997

Chancellor Helmut Schmidt
Honorary Chairman
InterAction Council
Tokyo, Japan

Dear Chancellor Schmidt,

I wish to thank you for your letter of 28 August 1997 and for sending me the very thoughtful and eloquent Universal Declaration of Human Responsibility proposed by the InterAction Council. I agree fully with your premise that with rights come responsibilities, and I share your commitment to non-violence, respect for life, justice, solidarity, truthfulness and tolerance.

I would be pleased to meet with some of the distinguished members of your Council with a view to learning more about the origins of and plans for a Universal Declaration of Human Responsibilities. My office will contact you to discuss this matter further.

Your leadership on these critical issues and your continuing interest and support of the United Nations is needed and deeply appreciated.

Yours sincerely,

Kofi A. Annan

II. China

First Conference on a Global Ethic and Traditional Chinese Ethics

Beijing, 10–12 September 1997

In order to express our viewpoints on a global ethic and human responsibility from the perspective of Chinese culture and to promote in common the cause of searching for a standard of global ethics, 24 religious and academic persons from Beijing, Shanghai, Xian, Wuhan, Guangzhou, Shenzhen, Haikou and Hong Kong, engaged in the study of ethics, religion (Confucianism, Buddhism, Taoism or Christianity), political science, law, economics, history, philosophy and literature, gathered to hold an academic conference in Beijing Da Jue Temple from 10–12 September 1997 and signed the following statement:

1. Basic Posture

In view of the close relationship between our widespread ethical crisis and many forms of human suffering;
the appearance of great efforts towards promoting dialogue among different religions and facilitating mutual understanding among various ethnic groups;
our sincere desire to improve the moral conditions of China and the world;
we salute the founders, signatories and promoters of the Universal Declaration Towards a Global Ethic, approved at the Parliament of the World's Religions in 1993; we respect

their sustained and unrelenting efforts and their genuine concern for the fate of the world and the plight of humankind.

We affirm that:

The above-mentioned Declaration is of great significance, as it attempts to seek the most basic ethical requirement of the already existing cultures and religious traditions, in an age which greatly needs to rebuild the moral foundation of the world order and to reaffirm and restate it in accordance with the conditions in which we now live.

The draft of the Universal Declaration Toward a Global Ethic discussed at several international conferences is a very worthwhile effort, which extends the scope of ethical discussion from religious to non-religious circles and goes beyond fundamental ethical principles by adding intermediate ethical principles to them.

The draft of the Universal Declaration of Human Responsibilities put forward by the InterAction Council is a very necessary move to give proper emphasis to the often neglected notion of responsibility, presenting human responsibility and human rights side by side.

2. *Major Themes*

In a spirit of egalitarian dialogue, the participants engaged in enthusiastic debate and discussion around the major themes of the Conference.

The participants explored the notions of 'traditional Chinese ethics' and a 'global ethic', noting the specific meanings and limitations of notions such a 'world ethic', 'global ethic', 'universal ethic', 'common world ethic', etc., as well as certain similarities in the human conditions which such an ethic addressed and the behavioural rules that it called for.

The participants were conscious of the complexity and diversity within 'traditional Chinese ethics' and realized that besides Confucian ethics this also included Buddhist ethics, Taoist ethics and other ethical conventions commonly accepted by Chinese people. At the same time they also discussed the changes and trials undergone by traditional Chinese ethics in modern times.

Much attention was given in particular to the relationship between 'traditional Chinese ethics' and the above-mentioned 'global ethic' in the conference discussions. The participants explored how traditional Chinese ethics could play its part in the concept of a 'global ethic'. Traditional Chinese ethics has always put a premium on 'harmony in diversity' (和 而不同) and 'the value of harmony', and this quest for harmony is the very basis for China's participation in the building of a 'global ethic'.

The participants recognized that it is necessary fully to understand and respect the different civilizations, ethnic groups, communities and even individuals with their diversity and distinctiveness; the essential feature of a 'global ethic' is the acceptance of a reasonable pluralism as its premise, so as to treat with equality individuals and communities which are different from ourselves. As expressed in the code of conduct, this is expressed in the basic laws like 'do not kill' , 'do not steal', 'do not commit adultery', etc., which have been handed down as unchanging core values of any culture or ethical tradition, and have been formulated in remarkably identical ways in different classical ethics or religious scriptures.

As for developing and constructing a universal ethical standard from the whole of human life past and present, the participants explored the possible contributions that Chinese tradition could make. The participants reaffirmed and restated the notions of 天 道 *(tiando*: 'way to heaven'), 天 理 *(tianli*: 'law of heaven'), 慈悲 *(renci*: 'mercy'), 仁 *(ren*:

'benevolence'), 民胞物與 (*minbaowuyu:* 'respect for life'), 生生 (*shengsheng:* 'compassion for all living things), 忠 恕 (*zhongshu:* 'loyalty and graciousness'), 中庸 (*zhongyong:* 'the golden mean'), 禮 (*li:* 'appropriateness in the social order'), 考 (*xiao:* 'filial piety'), 良知 (*liangzhi:* 'conscience'), 惻隱 *(ceyin:* 'compassion'), 知 恥 (*zhichi:* 'sense of shame'), 貴義 (*guiyi:* 'value of righteousness'), 重行 (*zhongxing:* 'emphasis on praxis'), etc. Such notions, as a resource of spiritual and natural values, may represent characteristically Chinese standards identical with a 'global ethic', or support and promote a system of global ethics. One case in point: we could use ancient teachings such as 'to do humanly is to be human', and 'do not do to others what you do not wish to have done to yourselves', to express the two fundamental requirements of a 'global ethic'.

The participants further pointed out that a 'global ethic' is an open system, and its conception is a starting point, not a final destination. We must continue the dialogue and the communication on a foundation of mutual tolerance and understanding.

3. *Some Hopes*

It is our hope that:
the conception of a 'global ethic' could be enriched and perfected, publicized and practised to benefit the establishment of moral relations between all people, nations and regions, and an international moral order;
the conception of 'a global ethic' could further absorb suggestions from religious, political, academic and other persons of different natures and cultural traditions;
the concepts of 'global ethic' and 'human responsibility' could eventually become the universal ethos of every citizen, community and nation, thus improving the moral condition of China and the rest of the world.

陈少明 Chen Shao-Ming　邓晓芒 Deng Xiao-Mang　何光沪 He Guang-Hu

何怀宏 He Huai-Hong　何 云 He Yun　黄克剑 Huang Ke-Jian

蒋 庆 Jiang Qing　李平晔 Li Ping-Ye　李秋零 Li Qiu-Ling

梁治平 Liang Zhi-Ping　刘军宁 Liu Jun-Ning　刘小枫 Liu Xiao-Feng

秦 晖 Qin Hui　汤一介 Tang Yi-Jie　万俊人 Wan Jun-Ren

王 焱 Wang Yan　王志远 Wang Zhi-Yuan　杨慧林 Yang Hui-Lin

杨熙楠 Yang Xi-Nan　尤西林 You Xi-Lin　余敦康 Yu Dun-Kang

张庆熊 Zhang Qing-Xiong　张志扬 Zhang Zhi-Yang　卓新平 Zhuo Xin-Ping

III. India

First Conference on a Global Ethic and Traditional Indian Ethics

New Delhi, 23–24 November 1997

Over fifty scholars and activists from various parts of India came together at the India International Centre, New Delhi, at a consultation convened by the Dharma Pathishtan on the 23rd and 24th of November 1997 to formulate an Indian response to the Declaration on a Global Ethic and the draft Universal Declaration on Human Responsibilities. The participants were unanimous in endorsing the relevance and wisdom underlying these two historic initiatives. The consultation noted that the Declaration on Human Rights has proved a blessing over the last fifty years by constituting an objective and compelling frame of reference by which to judge and restrain oppressive regimes.

In the light of the emerging global scenario, there is an urgent need to counterbalance the preoccupation with human rights with a corresponding emphasis on human responsibilities, if we are to secure the basis for making equal rights real and meaningful for all people. This is indeed a significant feature of the Constitution of India as is evident from Article 51(A). A notable virtue of the draft Declaration is that it places the global community – the Earth, humankind, the community of nations taken together – at the forefront, and balances thereby the hitherto selective emphasis on parts. It is highly commendable that this

Declaration boldly roots itself in the common heritage of all religions, and avoids the tendency to accommodate various religious lobbies by balancing one idea taken from a religion by another from a different religion. The draft Declaration is, in short, a significant landmark of our emerging global awareness and the enlarged sense of our universal inter-dependence.

It was felt that as Declarations by themselves do not suffice to ensure observance, once the Declaration is adopted, groups which have worked to mobilize endorsements for it should set up devices or organizations to monitor adherence to it – a good parallel is the effect which organizations dedicated to human rights and the care of the environment have had on translating Declarations on those matters into reality. The groups for monitoring the new Declaration must ensure that compliance is uniform – by all countries, groups and individuals. One of the features which has caused great disaffection in the poorer and weaker parts of the world is that Declarations are being used to perpetuate an unequal order: demands are made for an end to atomic weapons, except that the enormous stockpiles with the dominant countries are to continue; demands are made for reducing trade barriers, except that the enormous protection given to farmers in Europe or the textile industry in the USA must continue; demands are made for reducing the poisonous emissions that are harming the atmosphere, except that the schedule has to be tailored to the convenience of those who are putting the maximum amount of the emissions into the atmosphere. So that the new Declaration of Responsibilities may have meaning, so that it may be embraced by all the groups must ensure that it is complied with equally by all.

Participants observed that as movements grow to ensure compliance, as groups grow which will invoke the Declaration to ensure a humane future in different parts of the world, different elements of the Declaration will become the focus of attention. This differential emphasis is to be welcomed, as the elements that need emphasis differ from region to region.

Participants observed that ethical principles which refer to and arise from the ethical domain alone may not be sufficient to ensure discharge of ethical responsibilities. It is spirituality, the dynamism of faith, which has through the ages empowered and spurred individuals and groups to live up to ethical standards. Participants recalled that the Eastern peoples are an essentially religious people. In India, by using the teachings of our religions, by endowing them with newer meanings, a number of reformers have awakened vast multitudes to what they owe others; they have inspired them to serve others and the community. Participants felt that it is in crystallizing this body of experience that we can best further the cause of spreading the message of the proposed Declaration. Accordingly, we propose to convene a meeting of different reform and religious groups to gather lessons in this regard. We expect to put together a volume encapsulating the Indian experience in instilling a sense of responsibility and service through religion; this will be our first contribution towards translating the Declaration into reality. The volume will also provide a bridge between the Declaration Towards a Global Ethic and the new draft Universal Declaration of Human Responsibilities.

Participants

Swami Agnivesh was the main person responsible for the preparation and staging of the conference. Where not otherwise indicated, the participants come from New Delhi.

Prof. Anwar Moazzam (Islamic Studies, University of Hyderabad)
Prof. K. C. Yadav (Gurgaon)
Prof. Tahir Mahmood (Chairman, Commission for National Minorities)
Dr Alice Jacob (Law Commission)
Prof. T. K. Oommen (Nehru University)

A.K. Merchant (Bahai's House)
Ven. Doboom Tulku (Tibet House)
Maulana Wahiduddin Khan (Islamic Centre)
Rtd Justice Rajinder Sachar
Prof. P.S.Baren Ray
Prof. Allauddin Ahmed (Vice-Chancellor, Jamia Hamdard)
Mark Tully
Prof. M. S. Agwani (Udaipur)
Dr Karan Singh MP
Ms Monica Fimpel
Prof. Yash Pal (Noida)
Sh. Arun Shourie
Ms Anuradha Gupta (Mussoorie)
Rev. Valson Thampu (St. Stephen's College)
Ms Susheela Bhan (Institute of Peace Research)
Pawan Gupta (Mussoorie)
Basheer Hussain (State Minorities Commission, Bangalore)
Mrs Hamida Habibullah MP (Noida)
Dr Sadhvi Sadhana (Achanya Sushil Muni Ashram)
Ms Jillani Bano (novelist, Hyderabad)
Dr Promilla Kapur
Dr S. K. Sharma
Dr Tuisi Ram
Ms Kamala Mankekar
Shri Amrit La (Noda)
Rtd Justice V. R. Krishna Iyer (Ernakulam)
Joseph Puthooran
M. P. Krishnan Kutty (*Times of India*)
Ms Rajani Tandon (Temple of Understanding)
Dr V. S. Lal (General Secretary, Synod, Church of North India)
O.P.Shah (India International Centre)
Dr Suresh Chandra Sharma (India Museum)
Prof. Riffat Hassan (Lahore, Pakistan)
Ms Malvika
Dr D. P. Goel
Prof. Sheotaj Singh
Shri Jagvir Singh
Fr T. K. Jhon SJ
Capt. Rudra Sen
Capt. Bodh Jaibharati (Faridabao)
Dr Rishi Nanda
Samsul Islam
Karan Sawhany
Dr K.P. Shankaran
Dr Surendra Kadiyan
S.P. Mohan

IV: USA

Letter from the World Press Freedom Committee and Reply by the InterAction Council

Committee to Protect Journalists
Commonwealth Press Union
Inter American Press Association
International Association of Broadcasting
International Federation of the Periodical Press
International Press Institute
North American National Broadcasters Association
World Association of Newspapers
World Press Freedom Committee

Reston, Va, USA
3 November 1997

To the UN Secretary General
Kofi Annan

Dear Mr Secretary General,

As representatives of the Coordinating Committee of Press Freedom Organizations, joining nine global free press organizations, we urge you to help head off a serious new threat to press freedom, contained in a proposed Universal Declaration of Human Responsibilities. A copy is attached.

With what we are sure are the best of intentions, world leaders comprising the InterAction Council seek United Nations approval by the General Assembly of codes of ethics to balance or restrict fundamental rights in contradiction to long-standing provisions of the 1948 Universal Declaration of Human Rights.

In a world where freedom and repression both exist, such an exercise at 'reconciling ideologies, beliefs and political views' –

if taken literally – can lead to unintended, negative consequences. To cite just one example, one person's 'discretion' in news can be another person's censorship. If truth is to emerge, there must be the liberty to debate and assert all points of view, even if some such opinions and reports are considered to be irresponsible.

Freedom implies the freedom to be wrong.

Every journalist should be truthful and responsible, but to legislate this – to suggest that there is one official truth – surely contradicts the Universal Declaration of Human Rights' statement in Article 19 that 'Everyone has the fight to freedom of opinion and expression ... through any media and regardless of frontiers.'

We urge you to closely examine the proposed Universal Declaration of Human Responsibilities, with a special attention to what its provisions could mean if taken literally. We hope you will agree that pronouncements that undercut existing human rights, such as are presented in this draft, should not be considered.

The proposed document seems to contradict its own assertion, in its Article 19, that nothing it contains may be interpreted as implying a right to negate any article of the Universal Declaration of Human Rights. Indeed, its Article 14, which says that freedom of the media 'must be used with responsibility and discretion', is incompatible with the Universal Declaration of Human Rights Article 19.

In an atmosphere of calls for revision of the Universal Declaration of Human Rights, this statement seems to undercut the strength and universality of the 1948 document.

Surely the way to celebrate the 50th anniversary of the Universal Declaration of Human Rights is to reaffirm its universality and to seek its full implementation – not to amend or rewrite it so that authoritarians may negate the fundamental freedoms it provides.

Sincerely,

signed James H. Ottaway Jr and others

InterAction Council   10 November 1997

Dear Mr Secretary-General,

You certainly have received the letter of the Co-ordinating Committee of Press Freedom organizations of November 3, 1997, concerning article 14 of a Universal Declaration of Human Responsibilities, proposed by the InterAction Council. Having heard very positive comments on our proposal also from journalists, we do not know how representative this letter is for the members of the nine Global Free Press Organizations. Nevertheless, we take the letter very seriously, and we sincerely welcome a serious discussion. Let me therefore respond to the problems raised by the letter with a few remarks:

Obviously there is a very basic **fundamental consensus** between the letter of the journalists and article 14 of our Declaration:

1. The letter very clearly affirms the responsibility also of journalists: 'Every journalist should be truthful and responsible.'

2. On the other hand, our Declaration affirms very clearly the freedom of the press. Surprisingly, the letter of the journalists does not quote our most basic text in this regard, article 14, which even sharpens the Human Rights Declaration: 'The freedom of the media **to inform the public and to criticize institutions of society and governmental actions ... is essential for a just society ...**' This is consonant with the whole intention of our Declaration. Already the first phrase of the preamble affirms: 'Whereas recognition of the inherent dignity and of the equal and inalienable rights of all

members of the human family is the foundation of freedom, justice and peace in the world ...'

3. We share therefore the basic intention of the journalists: that existing human rights are not to be undercut, and that no article of the Human Rights Declaration has to be negated, weakened or restricted.

4. We are therefore convinced that a Declaration of Human Responsibilities would not be a threat to press freedom but, on the contrary, a support and deepening of press freedom. Certainly the journalists share our conviction, as expressed in our preamble, that '. . . the promotion of human rights depends on the readiness of men and women to act justly'.

Consequently, according to the affirmation of the journalists' letter that 'every journalist should be truthful and responsible', it cannot be contradictory to the freedom of press if we in our Declaration mention this responsibility of the media **explicitly**. We also mention explicitly the obligations of other important groups in our society, which are not exempt from general ethical standards, like politicians, public servants, business leaders, scientists, writers, artists and the representatives of religions.

It is probably the basic misunderstanding of the journalists who are responsible for this letter, to think that our proposal implies that the United Nations should 'legislate' this responsibility. Everybody knows that already the Human Rights Declaration is not a law in the strict juridical sense with sanctions, etc., but it is a moral appeal to individuals and institutions. **A Declaration of Human Responsibilities is even more a moral appeal** because as we declare, 'a responsibility to foster a better social order ... cannot be achieved by laws, prescriptions, and conventions alone'.

To make this responsibility explicit is especially important in a time when the increased power of the media also increases the danger of abuse of this power. The press itself reported many times on all sort of complaints in this regard, and recently in the context of the violent death of the Princess of Wales, there was a global consensus about the abuse of the freedom of press by certain photographers, journalists, newspapers and other media.

Precisely **because we reject censorship, we ask for a declaration of the responsibility also of journalists.** Certainly, this letter is right in affirming: 'Freedom implies the freedom to be wrong.' Evidently, also journalists have the right to be wrong, but nobody, not even a journalist, has the right intentionally to falsify facts and to degrade human beings. That is the reason why our article 14 affirms: 'Freedom of the media carries a special responsibility for accurate and truthful reporting. Sensational reporting that degrades the human person or dignity must at all times be avoided.' In this sense, we say that the freedom of the media 'must be used with responsibility and discretion'.

It is therefore quite obvious that the comment 'reconciling ideologies, beliefs and political views' (which is not a part of the Declaration, but only of the introductory comment) can in no way mean to balance freedom and repression. But it means, schematically speaking, that the insistence on rights, as above all in the West, has to be complemented by the insistence of obligations, as often repeated in the East.

Our general view is supported by the Declaration of Human Rights itself, where we find in article 29 a clear affirmation, 'Everyone has duties to the community in which alone the free and full development of his personality is possible.' And the same article explicitly states, 'In the exercise of his rights and freedoms, everyone shall be subject only to such limitations as are determined by law solely for the purpose of securing due recognition and respect for the rights and freedoms of others and of meeting the just requirements of morality, public order and the general welfare in a democratic society.'

At the end of this rather extended answer to the difficulties of the World Press Freedom Committee, let us express, dear Secretary-General, our deep desire to have also the support of the National and International News Media Organizations in order to guarantee and deepen the freedom of the press. That is the reason why we are sending a copy of this letter to its Committee.

With our highest esteem,

Helmut Schmidt   Malcolm Fraser   Kiichi Miyazawa

Editor's note

The InterAction Council can feel fully confirmed in its reply by the new 'Code of Practice' which has been worked out by the Press Complaints Commission (PCC) on the instructions of the British Government after the tragic death of the Princess of Wales.* Here are some central statements which confirm and make concrete the comments in the IAC letter quoted above:

'All members of the press have a duty to maintain the highest professional and ethical standards. This code sets the benchmarks for those standards. It both protects the rights of the individual and upholds the public's right to know. The Code is the cornerstone of the system of self-regulation to which the industry has made binding commitment. Editors and publishers must ensure that the Code is observed rigorously not only by their staff but also by anyone who contributes to their publications.

It is essential to the workings of an agreed code that it be honoured not only to the letter but in the full spirit. The Code should not be interpreted so narrowly as to compromise its commitment to respect the rights of the individual, nor so broadly that it prevents publication in the public interest ('the public interest' is defined specifically in an appendix to the Code). It is the responsibility of editors to co-operate with the

PCC as swiftly as possible in the resolution of complaints.

Any publication which is criticized by the PCC under one of the following clauses must print the adjudication which follows in full.

1. Accuracy

(i) Newspapers and periodicals must take care not to publish inaccurate, misleading or distorted material including pictures.

(ii) When it is recognized that a significant inaccuracy, misleading statement or distorted report has been published, it must be corrected promptly and with due prominence.

(iii) An apology must be published wherever appropriate.

(iv) Newspapers, while free to be partisan, must distinguish clearly between comment, conjecture and fact.

(v) A newspaper or periodical must report fairly and accurately the outcome of an action for defamation to which it has been a party.'

Then follow the other fifteen articles, the headings to which are given here:

2. Opportunity to reply
3. Privacy
4. Harassment
5. Intrusion into grief or shock
6. Children
7. Children in sex cases
8. Listening devices
9. Hospitals
10. Innocent relatives and friends
11. Misrepresentation
12. Victims of sexual assault
13. Discrimination
14. Financial journalism
15. Confidential sources
16. Payment for articles

*Information on the 'Code of Practice' is available from:
Press Complaints Commission
1 Salisbury Square
London EC4Y 8AE   E-mail: pcc@pcc.org.com.

Part Three: Conclusion

Two Declarations: A Comparison

HANS KÜNG

At first sight the Declaration Toward a Global Ethic of the Parliament of the World's Religions and the Declaration of Responsibilities of the InterAction Council seem very different. However, closer inspection will reveal the same conception behind the two declarations, expressed in basic approach, structure, content and formal criteria.

1. The **1993 Declaration Toward a Global Ethic of the Parliament of the World's Religions** is a document produced by religiously motivated people who see themselves as representatives of the religions of the world. They in no way claim to be 'better' than other people, indeed to be 'saints'. But they are all united by a conviction proved over a long life that the empirical world as we have it is not the final, supreme, 'absolute' spiritual reality and truth. Nevertheless the question of the basis for ethical norms is not answered by reference to a transcendent reality, but deliberately left open.

As the first document of this nature in the millennia-old history of religion, this Declaration necessarily had to be quite a long one: in its different sections it begins each time from the situation as it is, the situation in the present-day world, and then formulates – first in negative and then in positive form – the fundamental ethical requirements. Finally it moves to what should be and gives examples of the concrete application of these ethical principles. Its language and style therefore could and indeed had to be variable, and contain both descriptive and hortatory, analytical and emotional elements.

However, the Chicago Declaration Toward a Global Ethic is **not** one of the numerous **enthusiastic religious proclamations** which speak a good deal about cosmic consciousness, global harmony, spiritual creativity, universal unity and comprehensive love and merely conjure up a spiritual vision of a better world. Rather, it seeks to take the economic, political and social reality of present-day highly complex industrial society seriously and therefore to speak in quite concrete terms.

However, this Declaration does not mean to be **casuistic moral preaching** either. It certainly is not afraid of stating inconvenient truths and requirements clearly – for example respect for all life or the requirement of justice – nor does it bracket out the sexual sphere. But it does not follow certain representatives of the religions who admonish with raised index finger and threatening fist, nor does it lose itself in a jungle of commandments and precepts, canons and paragraphs. A priori it had to leave aside questions which are disputed in all nations, cultures and religions like contraception, abortion, homosexuality and euthanasia.

2. The **1997 Declaration of Responsibilities of the Inter-Action Council** is a document produced by statesmen who regard themselves as representatives of their nations. They certainly do not all claim to have acted morally at all times during their periods of active office in government and never to have failed; but they are united by an experience in decades of political activity which is both positive and negative, namely that in any political calculation of a policy which is to be effective in the long term, ethical judgment cannot be dispensed with. Since with their proposal for a Universal Declaration of Human Responsibilities these statesmen primarily seek to address the United Nations, their own peoples

and governments, their proposal takes the 1948 UN Universal Declaration of Human Rights as a model. Consequently, like that declaration the present declaration needed to be formulated briefly and 'legalistically'. Moreover the style of its language resembles that of official UN documents.

However, this Declaration of Responsibilities is **not** one of those countless **political manifestos** which pursue quite specific strategical aims of states and governments and claim validity only for this historical moment. It has the character of an abiding moral appeal, though it is meant to provide as much support as possible for efforts towards a just economic, social and environmental order. However, the declaration does not lose itself in questions of world policy and economic policy. In particular it has to leave aside explosive problems of today like the Middle East conflict, the resolution of the debt crisis, or the formation of a global framework for financial markets.

However, the Declaration of Responsibilities is **not a duplication of the Declaration of Human Rights** either. Were it only to repeat the articles of the Declaration of Human Rights in the same or other words, it would be superfluous. But it does seek to give effective ethical support and reinforcement to the UN Declaration of Human Rights, which is constantly ignored, violated and by-passed to such a terrifying degree. An ethic is more than law, and ethical obligations are more than legal obligations.

That, then, is a brief sketch of the differences. But what of the one ethical conception of the two documents?

3. **Both declarations** are about a **basic social consensus** in respect of existing binding values, irrevocable criteria and basic personal attitudes without which any community sooner or later is threatened with a state of anarchy or a new dictatorship. Both documents are about an elementary **ethic of humankind** or a **global ethic**.

Both declarations are addressed to **believers** and **non-believers**. They can be endorsed by theologians and philosophers, mystics and agnostics, Christians and members of other religions. They are not just aimed at intellectuals or educated people but at all men and women, in any of the world's regions or religions.

Both declarations are not typically 'Western' enterprises – a criticism which has often been levelled against them by Asian nations and cultures. Rather, they are based on an understanding of responsibility and obligation fundamental to Asian traditions and thus also formulate **fundamental requirements of the Asian cultures and religions.**

Both declarations have **the same structure**: they begin from the significance of a minimum of shared ethical principles for a better world order. Then they formulate the basic requirement of any human ethic: 'Every human being should be treated humanely.' Combined with this is the Golden Rule which applies to individuals and communities, nations and religions: 'What you do not wish to be done to yourself, do not do to others.' Finally they make concrete the four elemental imperatives of humanity which appear in all the great religious and ethical traditions of humankind: here the Declaration of Responsibilities presents the positive formulations before the negative ones.

Finally, both declarations have **the same content**: they not only agree word for word in respect of the basic requirement of humanity and the Golden Rule but also proclaim the same four irrevocable ethical directives – with insignificant variations in concrete formulations and applications: non-violence and respect for life, justice and solidarity, truthfulness and tolerance, mutual respect and partnership.

Thus the two declarations also fulfil the same **formal criteria**:
– They are **related to reality** and see the world realistically as it really is, not just as it should be;

146

– They penetrate to the **deeper ethical level** and do not remain hung up on the legalistic levels of laws, codified rights and paragraphs which can be contested, or on the political level of concrete proposals for solutions.

– They are **generally understandable,** avoid technical arguments and academic jargon and make use of a language which at least the average newspaper reader can understand, and this has facilitated the numerous translations into a great variety of world languages.

– They are both capable of **gaining a consensus,** and avoid statements which would be repudiated *a priori* by certain ethnic or religious traditions, together with condemnations which could be understood as violations of religious feelings. They presupposes that any reasonable person of good will can assent to this concretization of an elementary ethic of humanity.

Conclusion:
There Must Be Criteria

MARION, COUNTESS DÖNHOFF

There was great pleasure and satisfaction when after the terror of the Nazi dictatorship in 1948 the United Nations proclaimed the Declaration of Human Rights. Certainly there were civil rights, for example the right to vote and the right to domicile, but there were no human rights beginning from a moral view of being human which put human dignity and inviolability at the centre.

Human rights guarantee life and physical integrity, freedom of the person, of faith and of conscience. However, there can be no talk of a real guarantee, for fulfilment depends on the readiness of particular governments and the good will of citizens.

Here there are many difficulties: the view of what human rights comprise has to do with culture and tradition, morality and religion. The view of the Western world begins from the individual, whereas in large parts of the Third World, in Africa and Asia, the solidarity of the family and tribal alliance is the most important factor.

In these countries, Westerners keep hearing the objection: 'Your human rights merely support your effort to gain supremacy. In former times, in the colonial era, you ruled us because you were stronger and we were weak. Today you are attempting to do so by trying to force your specific view of human rights on the whole world.' They think that such Eurocentrism is inadmissible.

Furthermore, they do so with some justification. Of course some of our criteria which relate to everyday bourgeois life are diametrically opposed to that world: for example, among us polygamy is a criminal offence, whereas in some Third World countries it is not only admissible but even desirable. In parts of the world beating is by no means offensive but customary. The number of strokes depends on the particular crime.

When a few years ago an American was among those caned in Singapore there was a great uproar in the United States over this violation of human dignity. So it is not easy to implement the recognition of universal human rights. If the problem is not one of civil rights but of human rights, then torture, terror and discrimination enter the discussion. And here the problems are far greater, since there is no authority with competence to inflict punishment beyond national frontiers.

Certainly in the meantime human rights have achieved the binding character of international law, for example with the European Convention on Human Rights and the establishment of the European Court of Human Rights; however, they cannot be enforced, as we have learned from the civil wars in Rwanda or in Bosnia. Sometimes people have even been able to mock the flood of moralizing with which the Americans, for example, accompany their call for the observance of human rights; here they are the ones who quite often work with 'double standards'. Where their interests are at stake and where strategic perspectives play a role, as in Iraq, human rights are taken quite seriously. Where this is not the case; where, as in Saudi Arabia, the issue is safeguarding oil supply, Washington happily looks the other way. And the continued use of the death penalty in America is not precisely in line with human rights either.

China, which in 1989 after the brutal suppression of opposition demonstrators in Tiananmen Square – at that time several thousand students and citizens were killed – incurred the angry contempt of the West, is now being treated with velvet gloves because of its giant market.

The Turkish Foundation for Human Rights reports that in Turkey, which has subscribed to all the international agreements against torture, since 1980 hundreds of thousands have been tortured and more than 420 people have been tortured to death. Here at any rate the Europeans have made the right decision: for the moment they are not prepared to accept Turkey into the European Community.

More than a hundred states have ratified and recognized the Universal Declaration of Human Rights. Nevertheless, torture goes on, and human rights and basic freedoms are constantly violated. In 1992 the West looked on silently as the Junta prevented elections in Algeria because it was clear that the no less brutal opposition would win them. After bloody fights between Islamists and the military a state of emergency was imposed; terror and counter-terror cost 50,000 human lives in the four subsequent years.

On a superficial inspection one might think that since even after the proclamation and acceptance of human rights there is still torture, terror and brutality, the many discussions and crises conjured up by this topic are quite superfluous. This is an error.

There must be criteria by which governments can measure their inadequacy, even if this only results in a bad conscience. There must be handrails by which citizens in this chaotic world can pull themselves along; even if human rights remain no more than an appeal, it is important to take them seriously.

Now there is another similarly ethical appeal which Helmut Schmidt has recently made in *Die Zeit*: following years of preparation by philosophical, religious and political leaders, a group of former state presidents and heads of governments from all five continents has decided that fifty years after the Declaration of Human Rights, a Declaration of Human Responsibilities is absolutely necessary to supplement it. This would not of course have any binding character in international law, but if the United Nations were prepared to proclaim it officially, then finally responsibilities would visibly be set alongside rights.

Helmut Schmidt's account was followed by a series of articles, some against and some for, which have also been published in *Die Zeit*. The final summary in his remarks is: 'No democracy and no open society can survive in the long term without the twofold principle of rights and responsibilities.' And further: 'The nations, states and their governments involved in economic globalization must work together towards a minimal ethical code; otherwise the new century could prove as full of conflict as the century which is now coming to an end.'

Perhaps the proclamation of human responsibilities – if that should come about – would remain as piecemeal as the human rights which were greeted with so much hope. But this illuminating appeal could shed such intense light on the web of greed, avarice and corruption that many people would accept it. Perhaps, too, this appeal could help towards establishing ethical values for civilizing capitalism.

Finally, every society needs ties. No community, not even a club or an association, can exist without rules of the game, without a specific consensus over norms of behaviour. A society which is not agreed on an ethical minimal consensus and which does not accept any general moral barriers will inexorably collapse over time.

But what can we do? First, we must be clear that an ethic of responsibility is acquired through the process of education at home, in school and in the community. In other words, the civil society neither establishes itself automatically, nor can it be enforced by orders from above. For the modern state with a foundation not in religion but rather in a collection of particular principles – 'the rule of law' – will not and cannot give ethical guidelines; however, it must be able to rely on civilizing forms and basic moral attitudes in society.